It is 40 years since we first m̶
Danny has spent his whole life ̶
He has campaigned on behalf o̶
and discrimination, religious persecution and modern-day
slavery, providing practical help and support for those
in need, wherever he has found them. In this searingly
honest book, Danny bares his soul, from triumphs and
joys to difficulties and disappointments, and the deep
pain of grief at the loss of his beloved daughter, Jessica.
You cannot read this book and remain untouched.

**Bill Hampson OBE, Founder, Epiphany Trust,
friend and fellow campaigner**

For nearly forty years it has been a privilege to work with
Danny Smith as he has fearlessly fought for persecuted and
down-trodden people. But pouring yourself out for others
doesn't make you invulnerable to formidable personal
challenges. It comes at a personal price.

Danny has been characteristically honest in sharing
his own story of grief, depression, how it feels to find
your faith challenged, and much more besides.

Danny's book about his daughter Jessica is not just an
honest story, but a story which will help all of us as we
face our own challenges and demons. It also reminds
us that when everything else had been emptied out of
Pandora's Box, the one thing which was left was hope.

**Lord David Alton of Liverpool**

I have known and worked with Danny Smith for many years. He is a selfless journalist and campaigner, exposing the cruelty and suffering of countless children around the world. As a new father and an investigative journalist myself, I know how important it is to find comfort from what you see in the world through the love you can give your own child. Danny lost that, he feels helpless, angry, and lost. He is a broken man. But this is not the read you would expect: yes, it is heartbreaking, but it also takes you on the heartwarming journey of fatherhood, and the inspiring journey of overcoming every parent's greatest fear. It is also a tribute to Jessica, an incredible human being, and wonderful daughter.

**Chris Rogers, Multi-award winning
and Emmy-nominated presenter and investigative journalist**


I have read hundreds of manuscripts and books, but this is one of the most unique, and it is also well written. Danny Smith's daughter Jessica, at a very young age, died in her sleep, hitting him with grief that impacted him beyond words. The total mystery of God's timing. But as a gifted writer, he got the words with much help from God to write such a book – and it's powerful. I have known Danny for over 55 years but feel I know him better after reading this. This is not just a book for people who have faced deep grief, but for all of us who want the reality of the human experience and the God experience.

**George Verwer DD, Founder, Operation Mobilisation**

Danny Smith's *Goodbye Jessica* is beautifully written. He movingly and courageously shares his life journey and the loving bond between father and daughter and the devastating loss he felt (and still feels) when his creative and compassionate Jessica unexpectedly passed away at the tender age of 22.

We all suffer some loss in life. My father recently died and I'm grieving his loss. But what really impacts me is that instead of blaming God or harbouring feelings of anger or resentment, Danny sets those emotions down again and again. As a result, God's presence is able to meet him in that place of deepest grief and despair, in a way that nothing else can.

Danny Smith has always been one of my inspirations. He and his amazing wife, Joan, have given their lives to advocating (with Jubilee Campaign) for those who are persecuted for their faith and for children at risk. They have poignantly set up tributes in India, the Philippines and Zimbabwe in Jessica's name, to complete her desire to help vulnerable children.

**Sarah de Carvalho MBE, CEO, It's a Penalty Campaign**

This impressive account rendered by Danny about the pain and suffering due to the death of his and Joan's firstborn daughter, Jessica, will leave an impact on any reader. His very personal and candid words cannot fail to touch any empathetic soul. Albeit this is a heart-wrenching tale of human/parental agony, there is an uplifting message to encourage all of humanity. A quote from the Book of Job (5:17-18) may be appropriate:

Blessed is the one whom God corrects; so do not despise the discipline of the Almighty. For he wounds, but he also binds up; he injures, but his hands also heal.

**Michael Horowitz, Barrister and Notary: private practice, Jerusalem, Israel. Former Prosecutor, District State Attorney's Office, Tel Aviv.**

The moment I opened the first page of Danny's book, I knew I was not going to get through it without tears. It is too raw, too personal, too painful – and yet in a powerful way full of the affirmation of the faith of Job, a faith that is utterly authentic and utterly real, that touches the very heart of our humanity and strips away so much that is trivial. Jessica was special and Danny walks us all through the inner pain of his grief and the deep mystery of his faith. We are all made richer by his sharing it with us. I have known Danny for 50 years as a friend, a creative entrepreneur, passionately focused on making the world a better place, especially for the poor and downtrodden. I have read his other books and followed his amazing achievements, but this is different, so different. Here in utter honesty Danny shows us what is truly valuable in life, a father's love for his first-born in joy and the terrible pain of loss. As Danny says: 'There are tears. There must be tears. But there is no despair.'

**Mike Wakely, Founder, Starfish Asia**

A very moving, very personal, account of love, loss and longing. Death hit the Smith family like a lightning bolt. Grief sets you apart. Trauma does too. Others can't follow . . . And yet I found the book full of love, truth and hope also. Thank you, Danny, for finding the courage and strength to write and publish this book. Thank you Joan, too. Although you may not feel it most times, it is a story of hope and humanity and of the One who invisibly holds us together. It's never goodbye, for those we love . . . and for those who are loved and found by Him.

**Alice Diamond, former director,**
**Jubilee Campaign Netherlands**


I first met Danny Smith nearly 40 years ago in Zurich when he was campaigning for the Siberian Seven. His compassion for those families trapped in the US Embassy in Moscow, and his passionate plea for help was one of the reasons I determined to give my life over to similar causes. Once I started reading *Goodbye Jessica*, I couldn't put it down. This book is an account of Danny's life and couples those two qualities of compassion and passion with those of love and determination. It is a wonderful tribute to his beloved daughter Jessica, but is so much more than that. Danny's very public vulnerability gives us a glimpse of the struggles often faced by Christian leaders as they strive to lead a ministry whilst having to cope with their own private and personal struggles. It is a book full of dreams fulfilled but also one of heartache, and unrequited grief. My personal aim after reading the book, is to be very much more intentional about writing meaningful notes and cards to friends who are suffering! Highly recommended.

**Mervyn Thomas CMG**
**Founder President, Christian Solidarity Worldwide**

This book was one I didn't want to stop reading. It prompted me to think about my own family and just how precious is our time together on the earth. It challenged me to face difficult questions while illustrating the substance of a father's love for his children.

Over the years, Danny has always intrigued me by his passion and determination for building the kingdom as well as his work in the ongoing eradication of human trafficking.

Learning about Jessica was truly moving; she was a bright and passionate woman who left us far too early. *Goodbye Jessica* tackles the greatest of human adversities a parent could ever face. As a father, it draws my attention to the mystery of pain so often discussed by Christians.

Many of us have seen grievous losses paradoxically granting a more profound closeness with our heavenly Father. Unsurprisingly, Danny and the family continue to practice their faith and to navigate the significant loss of Jessica; my heart goes out to them all. Hebrews 11:1 tells us: 'Now faith is the substantiation of things hoped for, the conviction of things not seen.' We look forward to being reunited with the Father, for the mystery to be solved and for the tears to be wiped away

**Christian Elliott**
**Global Development Officer, The A21 Campaign**
**2020 UN Media Award for Can You See Me**

# GOODBYE JESSICA

## A Father's Journey Through Grief

### DANNY SMITH

malcolm down
PUBLISHING

Danny Smith has dedicated profits from this book to tributes set up in memory of Jessica. (All donations to Jubilee Campaign.)

I wish I could name each one who touched my life over this season: family, friends, trustees, church members, colleagues, partners, Jubilee Campaign supporters . . . You know who you are and have my affection and appreciation. Thank you for standing with me and my family. Your support has meant so much to us.

I'm grateful to Ali Hull for her immense contribution, taking the book from start to completion with smart navigation and editorial expertise. Malcolm Down understood what I was going through and made the process easy. Thanks also to Sarah Grace. Hayley Kyte, Suzi Hull and the design team at Hullo Creative were brilliant. www.hullocreative.com

With this book, I give Jessica her place in the world.

# Contents

# Introduction

The world changed the day I held Jessica in my arms.

A wriggling bundle of arms and legs, crinkly wrinkled skin, the determined twist of her body, the streaks of black hair across her head, translucent twinkling eyes that seemed to peer into deep space. And that wail, that very distinctive wail.

The maternity nurse at Queen Mary's Hospital Sidcup thrust her towards me without warning. I don't think she'd noticed the look of terror in my eyes. This was the nearest I'd been to such a tiny child in the thirty-eight years I'd lived on this earth.

I was about to ask her what the correct way of holding a just-born baby was. But I didn't get the chance. Before any words were spoken, my arms reached out and I was holding 7lb 12oz of living flesh, snuggled cosily in a towel.

I looked down and saw my daughter clearly for the first time. My heart melted. This child was the most beautiful creation I had ever seen. I couldn't take my eyes off her. I instinctively knew what to do and cradled my daughter in my arms. Together, we paced the floor of the maternity room for the next few minutes.

I couldn't stop smiling.

'I love you,' I called out loud to her. I must have repeated those words a thousand times or more. 'You're beautiful,'

I told her repeatedly. I wanted to cry out to the world, till my lungs burst. In that enchanted moment, I understood what joy meant.

When the time came to pass her back, she was nestled in my arms. I didn't want to let her go, cherishing our last few seconds together.

She was born at 2:26am on Wednesday 27 February 1985.

I left the hospital in Sidcup about forty minutes later to drive the six and a half miles back to our home in Abbey Wood in South London. 'I'm a father!' I yelled aloud, inside the car. I wanted to contact everyone I knew with this spell-binding news. I couldn't contain my excitement. In my head, I composed a list: my mother; my cousins scattered across the country; Wanno in Holland; Roley in Jerusalem; George Verwer, my mentor and friend, always there for me; Peter Benenson, the founder of Amnesty International, our family friend who'd spent hours talking to me about justice issues; my colleagues at the Siberian Seven campaign that I'd been immersed in for the last three years; the Siberians themselves, Timothy Chmykhalov first; the list ran and ran. I couldn't wait to tell them that I was a father and how beautiful my daughter was. I was going to . . .

ZXYKMYWTWZZ!KRACHUNK!

I heard the metallic crunch before I knew what was going on. It took a few seconds to hit me: I had crashed into a car at the roundabout on the border of Sidcup and Welling. It was early morning and there were virtually no cars on the road – except the car in front. In the clear moonlight, I saw the driver and a passenger get out of their car. They seemed agitated as both headed towards me.

'I've just become a father,' I blurted out. These total strangers were the first to get the news. It wasn't how I imagined delivering my message to the world.

Perhaps they didn't want to get further entangled with this wild-eyed crazy looking person with a deranged smile on his face. We exchanged insurance information, and I drove home with a semi-detached front bumper that caused a creaking groaning noise which probably woke up our neighbours.

I hardly slept and early that morning started on my list of calls to family and friends. But I couldn't wait to return to Queen Mary's. After fixing the bumper with wire, rope and thick Sellotape, I turned the car around and headed straight back to Sidcup. I found the ward and located the bed with the legend: Joan Smith.

There was a curtain around Joan's bed, and she was lying down, awaiting the return of a nurse who had been attending to her. There was a cot next to her bed. I drew the curtain back and spoke to Joan, reaching her side in a few seconds. I entered her enclosure from the left and as I passed my daughter, I could tell she was awake. I kept my eyes on the cot as I strode past.

My daughter turned her head and followed the sound of my voice. She hadn't been out in the world for twenty-four hours, but she knew one thing: the sound of my voice. Apparently, there's no proof that babies can distinguish their father's voice at birth. But my daughter recognised who I was. She'd heard my voice for nine months, and I'd told her a thousand times that I loved her just a few hours ago. She knew I was her father. And she was my beloved daughter.

Now, my world has changed once more because I can no longer feel her touch or hold Jessica in my arms. Never again will I hear her voice in this living world, or see her dazzling smile, or sense her come up behind me and cover my eyes with her hands, or receive a card from her with the words 'First Born', or feel her grip on my arm as we navigate traffic crossing a busy street in London, or see her name come up on my phone, or recognize that familiar excitement, 'Dad! Guess what?'

And here I am, in this room at dusk, with light fading as the day draws to an end. The cold steel thick darkness of the night awaits, while I embark on this mission to prepare a tribute to my beloved daughter, struggling to find words that will sustain me on this journey, as I steady my heart to say:

Goodbye Jessica . . .

PART ONE

# TRIBUTE

# First Born

*1921 – 1985*

When Jessica was born, it felt as if I was being born, almost as though I was being remade, and my life was starting over.

This child, Jessica, defined my identity as a father for the first time. She pointed me to where I belonged in God's kingdom and showed me who I could become. I was no longer a solitary man, since Joan and I had become a couple. The form of our family was being moulded into a different design and a new shape was being created. We were now parents. I was a father.

I knew very little about my own father. When I was growing up (in India), I'd never called anyone 'Dad' or used the word 'Daddy'. My world revolved around my mother, Eileen, who raised me.

My grandmother, Effie Macmarquis, was a vivacious personality from a Scottish/Irish family. She was an accomplished pianist who performed and organized concerts for the troops in India, during the British Raj. Effie was a divorcee with a young son, Jack, when she caught the eye of a dashing Irish army officer,

Captain Richard Elvidge, of the South Wales Borderers. Romance blossomed for the soldier and the musician, and marriage followed. After completing his term of service, Captain Elvidge settled with his new family in Crickhowell, Wales, and managed the estate of his commanding officer, Lord Glanusk. It was here that my mother, Eileen Alice, was born on 18 February 1921. Lord Glanusk was named as her godfather.

But Captain Elvidge lost all his money in a secret business deal that collapsed, and he died of shock. His widow, Effie, decided to return to her family, so in January 1926, with four-year-old Eileen, and her stepbrother Jack, she set sail from Liverpool on the *City of London*, bound for India. Effie's father, John Macmarquis, was the superintendent of the British military cantonment in Indore, an influential man in the city, who'd been honoured for many years of loyal service to the British Empire.

Meanwhile, my father, John Walter Smith, an Anglo-Indian, lived in Howrah, an industrial city on the west bank of the Hoogly River. Howrah was a twin city to Calcutta (Kolkata from 2001), the country's oldest port, once considered the cultural capital of India.

My parents met at a badminton club run by the Methodist church in Calcutta. Despite my grandmother's disapproval, the headstrong Eileen plunged forward with the wedding in 1946. But the marriage was doomed from the start and Eileen and Walter separated before I was born in December of that year.

My first and earliest memory is of a fight in the street. My mother was pushed against a wall while a crowd of onlookers gawked at this spectacle of domestic violence. Walter had seen his estranged wife and child at the New Market in Calcutta and attempted to grab me. He would have succeeded but a policeman witnessed the attempted abduction. He protected my mother and prevented my father from kidnapping me. Walter later surrendered custody and agreed financial maintenance for his son; in exchange, Eileen dropped court proceedings. He broke the deal and never paid any childhood expenses.

I was raised by my mother, a single parent with an undiminished strength of purpose to give me the best childhood possible. And she did.

My mother worked hard so that I could have a good life. Eileen rose before dawn to travel to her first job where she took shorthand dictation for a local business. She returned home in time to join me for breakfast, then left for her day job; she was a highly regarded secretary, and at one point worked as a personal assistant to the head of J. Lyons, the largest tea trader in India. During the day, I was under the supervision of my grandmother; as a former head teacher, she was stern. My mother spent the evening playing with me. After I was put to bed, she got to work typing up her notes from the first job of the day; that morning's dictation would be delivered at dawn the following day. I never realized the pressure she was under or her intensive workload and punishing schedule.

At the time, our household was comprised of mum and me, my grandmother, Effie, her brother, Charles Macmarquis, and his two youngest children, Betty and Pam. We lived in a rented top floor terraced flat in a six-storied building on Lower Circular Road, about fifteen minutes from the town centre.

I went to one of the best schools, La Martiniere, conveniently located opposite our building. I was teased occasionally because I came from a single parent home. One day, I overhead someone say, 'Danny Smith doesn't have a father. He's a bastard.' I had never heard the word used outside of a curse. I never told anyone about the incident.

My mother made up for everything. She was both mother and father to me. She conjured up a perfect world where everything I wanted magically appeared, and I never lacked for affection. I grew up thinking I could attempt anything in life and achieve whatever I set my mind to. Occasionally I wondered what it would be like to have a father.

One of my childhood games was to dream up someone else as my father. My mother had known an American soldier called William Elliott. This captivated me because I'd read about the Hollywood actor William 'Wild Bill' Elliott, the star of westerns such as *The San Antonio Kid* and *Tucson Raiders*. I made her scrutinize Wild Bill's picture, hoping for a resemblance. I would daydream about hunting down rustlers on a Texas ranch, and shoot-outs in smoky saloons. One day, I posed this question to my mother, 'If you had married Wild Bill, would I be exactly the same person I am today?' I don't recall her reply.

My favourite choice for a dad was always my cousin Freddy Macmarquis, the son of Uncle Charlie. Freddy was over six-foot-tall, with a Nordic appearance, pale skin, sandy hair and grey eyes. He had movie star looks and heads turned when he walked down the street. He had this laidback, ready for anything attitude to life. He played the guitar and sang songs by Hank Williams. He was a driver on the railroads but made a name for himself as a boxer; India didn't send a boxing team to Hitler's Olympics in 1936 so Freddy never went to Berlin, though he had been selected. I perched on Uncle Charlie's shoulders and watched Freddie in the boxing ring. He was a welterweight and usually won with a knockout. I loved going out with Freddy because people recognized him.

My parents were reconciled once when I was about ten, but it didn't last. A few years later, my mother heard my father was ill and took me to visit him. We arrived unannounced at the front door of the ground floor flat in Howrah, where he lived with his parents. When his mother saw both of us, she slammed the door shut. I wanted to leave but my mother spoke through the closed door, pleading with Walter's parents for his son to be let in. Finally, the door opened slightly. I was allowed in, while my mother was forced to stand on the street.

My father was in a darkened room resting under a mosquito net but woke up. After that, I saw him a few times over the years, but I can't recall any moments of intimacy or affection. He gave me some money towards a blue Claud Butler racing cycle, and explained the rules of cricket using match sticks to distinguish the teams. My mother told me his favourite song was 'I'll take you home again, Kathleen'. The song had a melancholic charm that provoked something within me when I heard it. Music became my way of remembering people and places and moments in time.

My mother struggled financially and was often in debt. I accompanied her to dimly lit rooms in dingy back streets as she paid off moneylenders. When she couldn't afford my school fees, I stopped attending La Martiniere – without any complaints from me. The principal was sympathetic and allowed me to return; the only requirement was that I earned my place. But school held little interest; I negotiated an exemption from Hindi classes, boasting of the accomplishment, and scrutinized *Melody Maker* more than any textbook. Eventually I did the fashionable thing and dropped out, much to my mother's disappointment. I intermittently attended a fine arts course, joined a friend's advertising agency, but mostly daydreamed about being a writer or an actor.

I was taken to church as a child and my mother rewarded me afterwards, for not fidgeting too much, with a visit to the toyshop to pick out a Meccano Dinky toy or a Roy Rogers comic. I was taught to respect people of different faiths and those with none. An unexpected encounter with George Verwer, the founder of Operation Mobilization (OM), a student Christian movement, led me to personal faith as a young teen. I travelled with OM in India and Nepal and became active in Carey Baptist Church in Bow Bazar. I didn't consider myself religious, but faith was embedded in me and I have carried this belief in God through life.

When I was a teenager, George tasked me with managing the OM Bookshop on Dharamtalla Street and one afternoon, my father's relatives dropped in. They told me that my father had died. I think they were surprised by my lack of reaction. I attended his funeral but didn't take any part in the service.

A few weeks after his death, my mother, looking solemn, asked me, 'Are you upset about your father's death?'

'No,' I replied.

'I've heard that you've been crying a lot,' she said.

What could she mean? It took a few minutes to unravel the mystery.

'I haven't been crying, mum,' I said. 'I've been laughing.' I'd been reading *Catch 22* by Joseph Heller, a black comedy about the Vietnam war. The book had me writhing with laughter, tears rolling down my cheek.

After becoming a parent, I felt a sadness about the life we'd never known as father and son. I never knew him in life, and I never missed him in death. Yet the absence of a father occasionally cast shadows throughout my childhood. It was like a nagging hook from a catchy commercial. You don't like it but can't stop it from getting inside your head.

\* \* \*

When we left India in 1970, Mum had hopes of reconnecting with her brother in Oxford and family in Wales, while I had dreams of heading to America. In the end, we settled in London, but I flew to the United States whenever I could afford to.

I didn't have a clear notion of my future direction in life. I worked in publishing while flirting with journalism, mainly to meet my favourite musicians. I had an interest in human rights: I was a founder member of Joan Baez's Humanitas UK; stood in the rain at a protest rally for imprisoned Russian dissident Vladimir Bukovsky; read all three volumes of Alexander Solzhenitsyn's epic *The Gulag Archipelago*. My last day job had been with World Vision International. I'd helped to set up their communications office in Europe and arranged the first BBC television documentary about the multi-million-dollar charity in the UK. I was preparing to write two books: Mike Porco agreed to work with me on a tell-all book about his legendary club, Gerde's Folk City, in New York, where many big stars started out, including Bob Dylan, who played 'Blowing in the Wind' there for the first time. An American publisher also sent me a book contract after learning that I'd talked with the reclusive Mr Dylan (in Los Angeles) and several musicians linked with him. Meanwhile, *Melody Maker* published my interview with Arlo Guthrie.

In April 1981, Peter Meadows, from the Christian conference Spring Harvest, asked me to lead a campaign to win freedom for seven persecuted Siberian Christians (the Vashchenkos and Chmykhalovs) in Russia. I took the part-time work because I thought it would be easy money, and liked the job because every day was different. There was no telling what might happen – including those unforgettable June days in Moscow . . .

The Siberians had lived for almost three years in a small basement room in the American Embassy but contact with them was forbidden. The Americans acted tough, probably hoping that the 'refugees' would leave. The seven feared arrest if they were evicted. I'd been given a contact at the Embassy but was told the Soviets bugged conversations in the building so he wouldn't talk freely inside.

The American official led me onto Chaikovskovo Ulitsa (street) and pointed out secret police (KGB) men as we walked. He was sympathetic and gave me directions to the Siberians' underground room. He also told me that the Soviets might think I had passed him confidential information on our stroll that couldn't be shared in the Embassy because of the electronic surveillance. 'Be careful,' were his parting words. What I didn't realize at the time was that my new friend was likely a spook. But thanks to him, I made contact with the Siberian families.

Over the next few days, I contacted every UK and US media organization in Moscow to persuade them that the Siberian Seven's forthcoming third unhappy anniversary (27 June) was a good hook for a story. Clearly, my activity wasn't normal for a tourist, and some suspicious incidents made me wonder if the KGB had mistaken me for a spy. I told the BBC's foreign correspondent, John Osman, everything that had happened. John thought that I would be arrested and said, 'Keep in close contact. If you haven't called, I'll assume you've been arrested, and I'll broadcast the news.'

I went straight from the BBC to the American Embassy, a place I assumed I would be safe. The Siberians were hopeful that the press would report their plight but concerned for my safety. Later, a US marine in the Embassy courtyard became enraged when I told him I was visiting the Siberians, and ordered me off the premises. I returned to the basement to pick up my coat and passport and to say goodbye. But the Siberians said the Moscow streets were dangerous for me and insisted that I should not leave.

The next few hours were tense because anyone could walk into their room, but before settling down for the night, we knelt on the cold floor. With the door wide open, scriptures were read, and voices raised in prayer. I can't remember a moment of greater vulnerability or such power. And then, incredibly, they created a hidden crawl space for me, and I slept in their tiny basement room on my last night in Moscow.

I kept our secret and only told a few people about the incident because they risked being expelled for breaking the rules if the story became public. That experience in Moscow was a turning point in my life. The Siberians had become my friends and I was determined to continue the campaign until they were freed.

* * *

I first caught a glimpse of Joan Edgar on 30 September 1981, on Fleet Street. Once the nerve centre of London's legendary newspapers, it has a publishing history that can be traced to the 1500s when William Caxton's apprentice, Wynkyn de Worde, set up a printing shop near Shoe Lane.

Joan was a former nurse from Cheshire and one of about ten girls who joined a publicity stunt to promote our campaign. Seeking media coverage, we organized a mobile birthday party for our absent guest – Peter Vashchenko, one of the Siberians. A lorry was decorated with ribbons, balloons, bunting and a huge cardboard birthday cake. Girls dressed in Russian costumes handed out freshly baked birthday cake as they walked beside the vehicle. We started at newspaper offices in Fleet Street, then moved on to Parliament and Downing Street, ending at the Soviet Embassy in Kensington. The party invitation (with a piece of cake) explained why Mr Vashchenko wasn't free to celebrate his own birthday with us.

The media loved the idea and were generous with their coverage. The television cameras wanted to record footage of the campaign director handing cake to a newspaper editor and I chose Joan to join me. It was only a few seconds, but we became an item on the lunchtime television news. Joan joined the campaign as my secretary for two months, but never left.

After the venture ran out of money and couldn't afford to pay for its office and operating costs, we had moved it into my home in South London.

I always believed the Siberians would be free but when it happened, I couldn't believe it. On 5 April 1983, the US Consul in Moscow telephoned me with startling news: 'Lida is going to be released. Can you meet her in Vienna tomorrow?' Without a second thought, I replied, 'Yes. Absolutely.' It was a secret and no one other than the key American and Russian officials knew about this sensational development. I booked my ticket on credit and flew the same day to Vienna. The acting US Ambassador, Felix Bloch, was friendly and surprisingly candid; later, he hit the headlines, accused of spying for the Russians.

Lida Vashchenko's arrival in Vienna on 6 April made headlines around the world. International TV coverage showed Lida and I leaving the airport terminal and walking to a rented black Porsche. I returned to Vienna in June to welcome the Vashchenko family, and one month later the Chmykhalovs. Eventually, all thirty-four members of both families (and their dog Volcano) settled in various cities across the United States.

By July 1983, the campaign was over. I had worked myself out of a job. But I still had one last item on my agenda, and a decision to make.

I invited Joan out to dinner at a restaurant in Greenwich. I crouched down as near to one knee as I could get without causing panic amongst the patrons of Brandy's, the trendy steak and cocktails bar set in the shadow of the Cutty Sark, and proposed to her.

I really wasn't sure what her response would be. I didn't have a job or a clear career path. I had no money in the bank. All my savings had been used on the campaign that I'd been focussed on for every single day of the previous three years.

But Joan understood all of this because she ran the office. I knew she was full of faith. I guess she was also in love.

Joan was selfless and had this purity about her. She was the least materialistic person I had ever known and didn't need 'things' to be happy. She offered help regardless of the sacrifice to herself. She would make a decision based on what was the best thing to do, rather than it being the easy way out or something that fitted in with her plans. She would do the right thing even if no one was looking.

It hasn't been an easy pathway for Joan and perhaps someday her full story will be known. Despite the adversities, she has this strength of character to remain true to herself and strong in her faith. There wasn't anyone I admired more. I had grown to love her. The thrill and wonder of when we first met stayed with me. We didn't have much, but we had each other, and that was enough.

I don't know the exact moment when I knew I wanted to marry her. I just knew I wanted her to be in my life and to never let her go. It had been a whirlwind romance and plans were taken at breakneck speed. There wasn't a moment to lose. This time, we had our own campaign to organize after we'd settled on 7 January 1984 as the date of our wedding. Four months to go.

\* \* \*

Timothy Chmykhalov was 16 when the Siberian Seven saga started in 1978. Before leaving Russia, he had married his childhood sweetheart, Tatiana. He had proudly introduced her to me on 18 July 1983, the day they arrived in Vienna.

When we learned that Timothy wanted to visit us and would be in the UK for our January wedding, I phoned him in Dallas, Texas and asked if he would honour us as my best man. His reply was to shout out to Tatiana. I'd never been good at languages, but it wasn't difficult to interpret this linguistic exchange.

When Timothy and Tatiana arrived, she was unwell, and Joan set up an appointment at the local health centre. The doctor couldn't understand Timothy's heavy Siberian accent, so Joan stepped in to help; she'd recently started a Russian language course.

A communication system was installed. The doctor asked Joan. Joan asked Timothy. Timothy asked Tatiana. Tatiana replied to Timothy who interpreted it for Joan. Joan relayed it to the doctor.

The questions yielded fruit: Tatiana was pregnant.

It was wonderful to be reunited with Timothy. We'd become close friends and worked on a book together. We'd arranged meetings in churches who wanted to meet the teenager who had forced the most powerful nations in the world to cut a deal. The last meeting on this mini-tour, days before our wedding, was at the Cobham Fellowship in Surrey.

On the drive to Cobham, Timothy told us of the struggles his family faced settling in the US. 'We don't know who to trust,' Timothy puzzled. 'We don't know who our friends are.'

I told Timothy that Joan and I had been discussing the same question. 'We know a lot of people but who are our real friends?'

At the meeting, the leader of the church, Gerald Coates, prayed for us. His words echoed our conversation in the car a few hours earlier. He said, 'God wants you to know who your friends are.'

Our wedding was held at the Dietrich Bonhoeffer Church in Forest Hill South London, and my bride looked radiant and beautiful. I couldn't have been happier when Miss Joan Edgar signed the register and became my wife.

This was the biggest day of Joan's life, yet she graciously chose the most inexpensive route for all our wedding arrangements. It was such gestures that defined her heart.

Our friends at the Ichthus Fellowship conducted our wedding service and offered to provide food for guests. We were grateful and relieved. We didn't have funds for 'Plan B'. Meanwhile I arranged to borrow a suit (and a ring) from a friend. We couldn't afford to book an official photographer so relied on friends with cameras. Peter Meadows' gift of a holiday in Cornwall became our honeymoon. The Cobham Fellowship took a collection that they shared between us and Timothy. It was such a relief not to start married life with a debt.

Gerald's prophecy about 'finding friends' resonated. We didn't have friends in Abbey Wood and little to keep us in the area. We were looking for a home for our family and our campaign. Joan made friends easily and people from the Cobham Fellowship expressed interest in our work. A move to Surrey sounded just what we needed. We drove to Cobham with high hopes. But we were in for a surprise.

We loved the village-feeling of Cobham but a quick glance at the estate agent windows gave us a sinking feeling. There were lots of properties for sale, it's just that we couldn't afford any of them. Weeks and months passed, as things followed a familiar pattern. Properties in our price bracket rarely came on the market and when they did, they sold quickly. We knew we'd have to move fast to hook one of the cheaper houses. Our snap decision to move from Abbey Wood had turned into a marathon.

\* \* \*

I discovered I was to become a father in 1984. Early one morning in July, Joan left the upstairs bedroom of our terraced house to go to the kitchen below where she'd left a pregnancy testing kit. Minutes later, I heard her yell. I think everyone on Overton Road heard her yell. I raced down the stairs like an action hero charging to rescue a damsel in distress.

'I'm pregnant!' she screamed. It was the loudest I'd ever heard her speak.

Joan was wild with excitement.

'That's fantastic!' I said, joining in the sense of thrill that engulfed us. After the first wave of fervour passed, the prospect of parenthood was unsettling; thoughts of my own father left me cold.

But, from the first second I looked down and saw my daughter at Queen Mary's Hospital, every question faded, and every fear failed. She was dazzling and exhilarating, and I never grew tired of watching her.

The unfolding of a new life for both of us was confirmed with the gift of our daughter on 27 February 1985. We named her Jessica Alice Siochain (a Gaelic word meaning 'peace') Smith.

There was a new creation alive in the world. Amidst the 4.8 billion people crammed onto Planet Earth in 1985, one more stepped up; not a statistic, no, not to me. This was my flesh. Mine. And when I spoke of my daughter, I took to calling her, 'My Jessica.'

I seized every opportunity to cradle her tiny body in my arms. Joan's childhood friend Lois Brown was to remind me later of how envious I was of my wife. I admitted 'I wish I had breasts so I could feed Jessica.'

When Jessica was born, it emphasized just how isolated we'd become in Abbey Wood. Not everyone gets another chance at a new beginning, and this was what the move to Cobham represented to this love-struck couple. We were tempted by offers of short-term accommodation in Cobham and reviewed options with our mentor, Peter Benenson, the founder of Amnesty International. 'Don't let impatience overrule common sense,' he cautioned.

When a two-bedroomed former council house went on the market, our friends phoned us, and we drove there the next day to view it. As we pulled up outside the building, I had a weird sensation: I could see myself walking up the driveway at some point in the future. I was ready to make an offer on the property before walking through the door. But I left the decision to Joan. Fortunately, she also liked it. It was all going well but we had one final hurdle: the mortgage. We owned the property in Abbey Wood, but to move to Cobham we would have to triple our mortgage, from £8,000 to £24,000. This didn't fit easily with our plans. We were trying to simplify our lives. The last thing we needed was to increase our outgoing costs. Still, we felt the move to Cobham was the right thing to do.

On paper, it was hopeless. We didn't have money for a deposit. And how did we intend to pay the mortgage each month? I was a freelance journalist without a steady income. I couldn't name a regular or potential employer. It was obvious that banks wouldn't queue up to offer us a loan. The pressure was on to a fix a deal quickly because we knew the property could be sold at any moment. Our friends said they'd pray for us, and we were praying. But what we needed was a mortgage. An appointment was made with a finance company. We bundled Jessica into the car and headed off to meet the broker.

The next few hours at the finance company seemed like a whirlwind. At some point, Jessica decided to sabotage the proceedings. She was hungry and let everyone know it. Our agent – the only female broker in the large open-plan office – took us into a private area so that Joan could feed our two-month old daughter. The agent talked to us but became mesmerized by our tiny baby. She spent most of the time playing with Jessica. The green light went on and we were waved past. Everything was pushed through without a second glance. The forms and questions became a formality. You're freelance? Fabulous! No regular employer? Oh, excellent. No proof of income? No problem! It was like an outtake from *Fawlty Towers*. We signed everything that was put in front of us.

Joan hugged me as we staggered out of the office punch-drunk, clutching an approved mortgage which gave us the right to make an immediate offer on the house.

Eighteen months after we'd taken a decision to move to Cobham, our prayers were answered. In July 1985, with Jessica just five months old, we completed the move. We knew that everyone's prayers played a part but had a hunch why a distracted broker approved our mortgage.

Jessica's performance art was a showstopper.

CHAPTER 2

# A Father at Peace

*1985 – 1995*

The house in Cobham was ... cosy but it was home, and we loved it.

We crammed our campaign files into one bedroom which became the office, with the overflow of books, leaflets and documents squashed into the living room where the photocopier took centre stage. Over the next few months, the office commandeered all the available space in our home, while my unpublished Dylan manuscript, Elvis memorabilia and *Rolling Stone* magazines were archived to the loft.

Jessica's toys mingled with our campaign materials. Something about my 'Free Nelson Mandela' badge captured her imagination and she took it to 'Show & tell' at the Rainbow playgroup set up by women from the church.

When Jessica needed space of her own, we moved her into our bedroom. This meant that Joan and I slept on the living room floor. We'd roll up our sleeping bags each morning to get the room ready for work, before the volunteers arrived.

After the success of the Siberian Seven campaign, we received several appeals for help. The first was from Timothy Chmykhalov, who explained why his wife Tatiana was upset: 'Tatiana's family have problems with the authorities in Siberia. We want them to join us in the West. Can you help?'

We were exhausted after the intensive three-year campaign but couldn't refuse Timothy. Our behind the scenes lobbying succeeded in getting Tatiana's mother and two sisters out of Russia. But, as asylum-seekers, they were stranded in Rome. Criminal gangs had easy access to shelters and there were rumours of refugee girls being trafficked across Europe. Such families didn't have any influence and were powerless to act, while the authorities turned a blind eye. Tatiana was worried that her sisters could become the next victims of the traffickers.

We investigated the risks facing Tatiana's sisters and eventually secured safe passage out of Italy for her family. It was exhilarating to watch things change so dramatically as a direct result of action we had taken. It felt as though the 'campaign' had never stopped. We used all donations for direct campaigning costs and took no salary. A Dutch television station appointed me as their London correspondent. It was easy work and the money had paid for part of our expenses in Abbey Wood, but Cobham in Surrey was different – and expensive. As the requests to help increased, I found it difficult to keep up with my Dutch media assignments. Gerald Coates's church contributed to our family expenses, but we struggled to make ends meet.

\* \* \*

On one of my visits to the Siberian Seven in Moscow, I'd smuggled a guitar past the watchful eye of the airport custom guards. It was for Valeri Barinov, a rock preacher popular amongst young people, in Leningrad (St Petersburg since 1991). Valeri's enthusiasm for rock music and his Christian faith had led to his arrest (in 1983). He was sentenced to two and a half years in a labour camp. We were worried that he wouldn't survive. So, the campaign was saddled and ready to ride again.

We still operated as the Siberian Seven Committee and one of the members, Bill Hampson, took the Barinov case to Liverpool MP, David Alton, who agreed to help. But David was a visionary. He invited us for lunch with Mike Morris of the Evangelical Alliance, among others; this group, along with Peter Benenson, became an informal board. David's plan was simple: set up a Parliamentary Adoption Programme and invite MPs to help prisoners of faith. David 'adopted' Valeri Barinov as the first case.

We organized the project but first things first: we needed a name. I settled on Jubilee Campaign. It reflected the biblical teaching of Leviticus 25 when a Year of Jubilee (every 50 years) declared prisoners and slaves released and pardoned, debts forgiven, land restored, and property returned to owners. It was essentially a redistribution of wealth. This idea of 'justice in action' encapsulated the mission in my heart and the work I wanted to commit my body to do.

At the same time, a friend from church paid for our first fulltime worker, Rosie McLaughlin, to join us, and offered his home to accommodate our growing office.

As Joan was pregnant with our second child, we moved the office on the morning after the invitation was made.

David Alton, at the time the Member of Parliament for Liverpool's Edge Hill, launched Jubilee Campaign in February 1987 in Parliament's aptly titled Jubilee Room. Over thirty MPs signed up to adopt prisoners of faith. The media covered the event, which was interrupted by a courier from Downing Street who handed over a personal endorsement from Prime Minister Mrs Margaret Thatcher.

There was success at home as well. One month after launching Jubilee Campaign, Joan went into labour. We headed straight for Epsom Hospital, but she was so calm, the nursing staff didn't believe she was in labour. 'I'm not leaving,' Joan insisted. 'I'm having a baby!'

Of course, Joan was right, and at 3:27pm on Tuesday 10 March, Rachel was born. There's no other feeling in the world like that moment when you hold your child in your arms for the first time, and the electric surge of joy was overwhelming when I cradled my daughter. For a fleeting moment, I was unsettled by thoughts of an absent parent from my own childhood, but it was quickly forgotten with the happiness of becoming a father for the second time. Rachel's birth made me feel that my life had meaning.

Joan noticed that I'd been wearing the same shirt as when Jessica was born. Later, it was washed, ironed and kept ready, in case it was needed in the future.

Two days later, I took Joan and Rachel home from the hospital. Jessica was delighted to see her mother again. She was particularly pleased with the gift of chocolates that her sister brought for her. One afternoon, she told Joan, 'I love Rachel. I'm going to buy the new baby some hair.'

* * *

Peter Benenson was a family friend who had a towering influence on my thinking and the mission of Jubilee Campaign. He had set up Amnesty International with the simple idea that a letter written by an individual had the power to bring change, and he still wrote a personal letter every day to protest against human rights violations.

He was equally concerned about issues nearer home and was a regular hospital visitor; he took an active interest in our family, and after learning that Jessica had trouble sleeping, he made several practical suggestions. On a visit to our home, he took a phone call from estate agents that confirmed the purchase of a property in Oxford. When he discovered we couldn't afford a holiday, he insisted that we take a break in this house, one that he planned to retire to.

David Alton's Parliamentary Adoption Programme proved effective and over a hundred MPs 'adopted' prisoners of faith who were persecuted for their beliefs. There were many significant breakthroughs as we took up cases in places as politically different as the Soviet Union, South Africa, Sudan, Ethiopia, Eastern Europe, Cyprus and Turkey, among others. We developed a brilliant team, each of whom, like me, raised their own support. With David's backing, Jubilee Campaign gained a foothold in the parliamentary fortress.

David took every opportunity to lobby for Valeri Barinov's release. We employed the tactics that had worked effectively for the Siberians: media, political pressure, encouraging prayer and action from the church. Mrs Thatcher raised his case during a visit to Russia and, days after her departure, the local visa office summoned him to collect his exit documents. But Valeri wouldn't be pushed. He told me on the telephone, 'I'm going to decide when I leave.' I thought it was risky but admired his courage.

Finally, in September 1987, BBC TV News broadcast the Barinov family's arrival at Heathrow Airport. The media coverage reported Jubilee Campaign's strategic role in his release.

\* \* \*

While I was energized by being at the heart of the campaign engine, I hadn't noticed that Joan faced a different kind of intensity. She was left to deal single-handedly with the stress of running the home without enough cash coming in, juggling the bills and trying to pay for the food shopping each week. At one point, we couldn't afford Ribena for Jessica.

Joan carried this pressure single-handed. There were several occasions when the money ran out before the end of the month. But there were days when she found envelopes pushed through the letterbox with pound notes inside. One month when things were desperate, we were sent a cheque for a rebate on my tax bill. It was exactly enough to get us through that month. Later, another tax rebate arrived. This time it was for Joan, which was surprising since she hadn't applied for one. It got us through another month.

I was focussed on the campaign, but equally enraptured by my daughter. I scribbled down special experiences with Jessica in my notebook, wanting to preserve the moment.

And there she was, aged three, sprawled across the living room floor, with coloured pencils and wax crayons, fired by a highly charged imagination. 'I'm making a gift for God,' she explained. 'I'm drawing a picture of a dinosaur.'

'Why a dinosaur?'

'Dinosaurs lived a long time ago,' she replied, without missing a stroke of colouring. 'God might have forgotten what they looked like.'

It snowed that winter, and every street in Cobham could have been selected for a picture postcard. Jessica sat on the window ledge of her room on the first floor, her jet-black hair reaching almost to her waist. Outside, the snow had covered the houses, trees and everything in sight. I walked over and hugged her. She looked directly at me and said, 'All the snow in the whole wide world is my love for you, Daddy.'

The wooden desk in our reclaimed bedroom faced the window overlooking the front of our house. One day, I found her at my desk staring at my IBM golf ball typewriter. There was a piece of paper in the carriage roller.

'Daddy, how do you use the capital button on this machine?'

I showed her how to capitalize the letter and glanced at the words on the page in the typewriter. It was addressed to Joan. The note read: 'Mummy I . . .' She wanted a capital L.

'It's OK Jessica, it's not a problem. Love can be written with a small "l".'

'No, it can't Daddy,' Jessica replied confidently. '"Love" is a very important word. I want it to be in capitals.'

That was Jessica. From an early age, she had a clear sense of what was important in life. She would decide what she wanted to do and find a way to get it done. That determination, drive and energy never left her.

I loved autumn with every tone of colour in the artist's palette on view. The leaves may have been dazzling while on the trees, but dead leaves on the ground demanded a work force.

I couldn't shirk my duties any longer, and one Saturday found me working in the front garden – a rare sight. Jessica joined me on garden duty. At first, she was an enthusiastic apprentice, and together we filled two waste bags of dried leaves.

'Daddy, who invented leaves?'

'God.'

'Not a very good idea. I wish they could just stay where they are.'

\* \* \*

Valeri, Tanya and their teenage daughters Zhana and Marina had accommodation in Chislehurst, but he spent most days with us in Cobham. I became his taxi driver. Our journey took us past Queen Mary's Hospital, where Jessica had been born, and I pointed it out to him. Over the next six months, I ghosted his autobiography. It was his story, but I chose the title: *Jailhouse Rock*.

While working on the book, I developed a severe throat infection. 'Come on!' Valeri said, in that infectious way of his. 'I will pray for you.' It was a short, simple prayer, conversational in style. He touched my throat as he prayed.

A few minutes later, I felt something physical stir in my throat, and shortly after that, it cleared completely. Whatever the infection was, it had gone.

Rachel didn't give her trust easily to people but allowed this long-haired Russian to pick her up, and felt comfortable in his arms. She started to suffer from recurring ear infections when she was about eighteen months old and, after repeated antibiotics, the doctor warned Joan that she'd require grommets if the infection persisted. Grommets are tiny plastic tubes inserted into the ear drum to enable children to hear properly. The operation itself usually lasted about ten to fifteen minutes but, without treatment, children can suffer lasting hearing loss.

Joan told Valeri that Rachel was on antibiotics for yet another ear infection, and that the doctor had said it was probably the final time he could prescribe the drugs. She didn't want Rachel to undergo the procedure but was worried that the antibiotics weren't touching the infection.

Valeri's reaction was to lift Rachel up, and to pray healing for her. Rachel stared at him while he prayed. Her condition improved from that day. When Joan returned to the surgery with our daughter, the doctor said the infection had cleared up completely. Rachel was never troubled by this condition again.

Valeri always made time for Jessica and she developed an attachment with him. He taught her to do a roly-poly. It was hilarious watching them rolling around on the living room floor. Jessica and I went to hear Valeri speak at a church on the south coast. During the service, Valeri spoke about Jessica. Then he picked her up and held her over his head so that everyone in the audience could see her. On the way home, she told me she wanted to give Valeri something, 'I love Valeri. Let's always be friends with him.'

\* \* \*

When Valeri's wife Tanya learned Joan was pregnant (in 1988), she said, 'A boy! Please, a boy!'

Late in the evening of 19 January 1989, Joan's contractions were coming fast and strong. 'We've got to get to the hospital now,' she insisted. 'Hold on,' I replied. She looked at me in bewilderment. I dashed into our tiny bedroom and scrambled into the shirt I wore when Jessica and Rachel were born.

A heavy fog had settled over Surrey that evening but our blue Citroen (a gift from a friend) got us to Epsom Hospital in record time. And without a speeding ticket.

It was such a joy to give Valeri and Tanya the news that our son Luke arrived half an hour after midnight on 20 January. When we brought Luke home from the hospital, Jessica, almost four, was captivated by her baby brother. She said, 'I'll fight giants for you, Luke.'

She adored her brother. One lunchtime, I was coaxing him to finish. 'Luke, eat your food or you won't grow into a big boy,' I commanded.

But Jessica challenged me. 'It's OK if Luke doesn't grow up to a big boy.'

'Why?'

'I want him to stay small and cute.'

Joan and I watched Luke at play with fascination. With two girls, there were girl-type toys everywhere, but our son uncovered everything that resembled a car, train or gun from every room in the house.

I had a special bond with Jessica as my first-born child. I didn't love Rachel any less and developed an abiding attachment to her. And I loved having a son. It felt that I had reclaimed something missing from my childhood, as an affection flourished between father and son.

The birth of Jessica, Rachel and Luke opened some undiscovered love in my heart as a father. I didn't know I had the capacity to love each child in this distinctive way.

Jessica and I spent many hours together and went on many adventures. Those were the happiest of times, days that make me smile as I bring them to memory. Jessica invented this game in the car where she moved her hand to the left or the right to decide the direction of travel. Driver and car obeyed her instructions.

One day we saw a rainbow stretched across the sky. Jessica said, 'Dad, let's follow that rainbow. Let's see where it ends.' She was the navigator, as always. And we drove. And drove. I can authoritatively report that the rainbow ends somewhere between Wandsworth and Wimbledon. I know. Jessica and I have been there.

I noticed Jessica staring at my hands on the driving wheel. She'd spotted that I didn't wear a wedding ring, and this upset her. Over the next few days, it became the hot topic of conversation. She made me promise to get a ring.

'I want you to wear a ring, Dad. I want people to know that you have a family, that you belong to us.'

* * *

Jessica's favourite book was *Home for a Bunny*, a gift from a friend to celebrate the arrival of her sister Rachel. It was her first choice as a bedtime story. She knew the text by heart. Sometimes, when I was busy, I would skip a sentence and start the next page in my rush to get bedtime over. Quietly but firmly, she would turn the page back and give me 'the stare'. That look in her eye said it all. Then she'd tap the page with her finger. No words were needed. I never succeeded in skipping a word or sentence from *Home for a Bunny*.

As a child, Jessica had a simple faith. When Joan couldn't find her car keys or was seeking a parking spot in a busy town centre, her response was, 'Let's pray.' To her, this was a natural way of dealing with problems.

The Cobham Fellowship prioritized relationships over meetings. They held one weekly service (on Sunday) that started at 7pm; and there were few activities for young children such as ours. Once a month, the church hosted a popular event, often held at the Surbiton Leisure Centre. The leaders expected me to sit on the stage even if I didn't take a part in the service. Jessica loved being on the stage with me. One Sunday, we arrived early, and Jessica led me to the front row. Before we could take our place, one of the organizers asked us to take a seat further back.

'I want to sit on the front row with my Dad,' she asserted.

'That's reserved for the speakers, Jessica.'

But she was undeterred. 'That's OK,' she replied.

And that set the pattern. It was accepted that if Jessica attended the service with me, we'd be at the front.

\* \* \*

Jessica was about four or five when she started coming with me to the campaign office and was fascinated by our campaigns. Whenever we moved, she was eager to see our new surroundings. After Sam Hammam invited us to use his premises at Wimbledon Football Club, she enjoyed exploring the pitch and the stands.

In December 1989, the uprising in Romania was headline news. Several years before this, we'd smuggled aid and supplies into the country for distribution through trusted church networks. When the revolt hit the headlines, we had unprecedented in-country contacts. As a result, the media featured us prominently, and this led to our contact with Olivia Harrison, the wife of former Beatle George Harrison, and Steve Brown, the music producer for Elton John, among others. Olivia and the other Beatles' wives, Linda McCartney, Barbara Bach and Yoko Ono, established the Romanian Angel Appeal and raised millions of pounds that was spent on refurbishing orphanages and projects that directly helped thousands of children.

Olivia and Steve invited me to serve as a trustee, and together we directed the project. Both Olivia and Steve were brilliant. One day, while faced with a decision, Olivia asked, 'What will help the most children? That's the right thing to do.' That was how most decisions were made. They asked us to run the operation with them and paid our team for six months. This was a turning point for Jubilee Campaign. It was the first time that anyone had received a salary and established a financial base for Jubilee Campaign. I was the last team member to go on the payroll.

It was a thrilling moment when Olivia first played 'Nobody's Child' to us. George Harrison had recorded the song with his friends from the Traveling Wilburys (Roy Orbison, Bob Dylan, Tom Petty and Jeff Lynne). I took a copy of the tape home and Jessica loved the song. One day she played it repeatedly while drawing a picture 'to help'. She dedicated the picture 'For the Romanian orphans. For the smallest baby.' I showed Jessica's picture to Olivia and Steve and we talked about how the song had inspired my five-year-old daughter to do something to help. The song (and later the album George organized) would go on to inspire people worldwide and raised a massive amount of money to help Romania's orphans.

In 1990, we started a campaign for Charles Bester, a young Christian who had been imprisoned in South Africa for refusing to serve in their military. Our petition calling for his release was signed by thousands, including anti-apartheid journalist Donald Woods and Sir Richard Attenborough.

Something about this campaign caught Jessica's imagination. She thought it was outrageous that he (like Valeri Barinov) was jailed for his beliefs. 'We've got to help Charlie.' She took the appeal to playschool and returned clutching petitions with barely distinguishable scrawled signatures. And at night, she prayed for Charlie.

David Alton lobbied everyone he could. About the same time, we took up the case of the Sharpeville Six in South Africa. They'd been found guilty under the doctrine of 'common purpose' of the murder of the deputy mayor of Sharpeville and sentenced to death by hanging. Armed with petitions and appeals, David and I walked from the House of Commons to the South African embassy in Trafalgar Square. The meeting with the diplomat didn't go well, but after a worldwide outcry, the Sharpeville Six's death sentence was commuted to 18-25 years in prison.

Jessica squealed with joy when I told her Charles had been released after serving 20 months of a six-year sentence. She probably didn't comprehend what it meant to be imprisoned or released. But she knew something had changed.

When Charles visited the UK, I arranged for Jessica to meet the young activist. She was so excited. On the appointed day, she'd developed an eye infection, but nothing could deter her. She said, 'I can't believe I'm really going to meet Charlie.' He was sweet with her and said the innocent purity of a child's earnest prayer had encouraged him.

Our friends Jim and Kitty Thompson arranged for me to speak at their church in Belfast and I took Jessica with me. It was the first time she'd flown in an aeroplane. She was about seven, a few years older than Jim and Kitty's daughters, Judith and Alison. The girls wanted their hair done in a particular style and, of course, Jessica knew what to do.

The Thompsons had given us their daughters' room where the beds were placed in an 'L' shape. As we settled down Jessica said to me, 'Dad, let's go to sleep holding hands.' And we did just that.

On our journey home, we waited in the departure lounge at Belfast's Aldergrove Airport. Jessica wanted to be the last to board, 'I don't want this to end.' But the ground staff insisted, and a stewardess escorted us onto the plane.

Jessica loved life. She wanted to climb to the top of every hill, explore every side street, try every toy in the shop. She studied the piano, enjoyed horse riding, a puzzle book (later Sudoku) was always close at hand, and every Saturday morning, I drove her to Stagecoach in Merrow for drama and dance classes.

\* \* \*

In 1993, we moved house: from Cobham to New Haw, about five miles away; that same year, Sam Hammam was preparing to sell Wimbledon Football Club and the office relocated to a hall in St John's Seminary in Wonersh, a tranquil village tucked away in the Surrey Hills.

I got to know some of the theological students and was stirred by the depth of their commitment. The students made friends with Jessica and allowed her to use their common room which included a ping-pong table and an extensive video library.

Jessica loved to explore the extensive grounds of the seminary and uncovered secluded gardens and pathways unknown to me. One day she told me that she'd seen a deer. 'It was just standing there looking at me.'

I could look at Jessica's face and see how much she adored life. She was a born leader with natural confidence. If a problem arose, she'd find a way to fix it. We visited Fullbrook School for Rachel's Open Evening. When we returned to the car park, our car had been boxed in. Jessica scribbled down the offender's licence plate and returned to the school. Minutes later, she returned with an apologetic driver who reversed out, and we left without any dents. Jessica had arranged for the car's licence plate to be announced. But she didn't just hope for the best. She waited until the car's owner was located and then marched the errant driver to the car park where we were waiting.

I loved Jessica's thick long black hair, cascading down below her waist, but we argued because she wanted it cut. It was difficult to maintain and limited her style options. One day Joan warned me, 'Jess wants to talk to you after work.' I rehearsed the negotiations during the day. What I would say. How we would barter. I'd make clear my position and explain why she must keep her hair long. The exchange went something like this.

'Dad, I'm cutting my hair.'

That was it.

Jessica was a natural entrepreneur. There was Jessica's Pet-Sitting Service, The Jessica Corporation, among others. She produced leaflets, calling cards and business plans, for her several ventures and enterprises. She'd set her mind on a market stall at Portobello Road. One day she sat me down very professionally and said, 'Dad. I've got a job for you. This is serious. I'm going to produce high quality original t-shirts. I want your designs to be the first we create. You must do your best artwork for me.' As she grew, the plans got bigger. She told me, 'I'll have my own factories making clothes I've designed. I'll pay my workers well and treat them fairly.' The Fairtrade movement had got going and I assumed this had been the instigator. When pressed, it became clear this was her own idea. She told me, 'This is what I believe.'

I think about those days a lot. The adventures and excitement of our time together. How I felt, that sense of contentment that absorbed me. I was a father at peace.

CHAPTER 3

# Teenager in Buffalo Boots

*1996 – 1999*

In 1996, Jessica decided to change the spelling of her name. She was now Jeska. But it wasn't just her name that was changing.

Overnight she became sullen, argumentative, insolent and secretive. She started to hang out with a new group of people. I was summoned when 'Dad's Taxi Service' was needed to get her from here to there. I'd be told to stop the car at a random spot. Yet, she wouldn't tell me who she was visiting or where she was going. She was swirling and twisting and testing the ground beneath her feet. Eleven, and a teenager.

Jessica was independent, strong-willed, and her fierce charge at life set up clashes at home. She thought she could do anything and wanted to do everything. Nothing had prepared us for her desire and determination to experience all life had to offer. She was moving at speed as she whirled at the edge of the cliff face. But she had her face to the wind and enjoyed the thrill of being alive. It seemed she could only find herself by overthrowing the old order. As her parents, we were worried by the hazards this emerging youth could face. We weren't ready for the fiery young rebel that she was turning into, nor the risks that we suspected that she was taking.

She rose to peril and danger. It had started when she was about five years old.

We regularly visited Ripley, a town that dated back to Norman times and is referenced in H.G. Wells' novel *The War of the Worlds*. One afternoon, we stopped by a field about a mile from the high street. On our way back to the car, we walked in single file. There was no pavement, and as cars whizzed by, Rachel and Luke held onto Joan's hands. Jessica and I led the way. We stopped by a bridge across a stream. In the distance, we could see the ruins of an ancient building; later, I learned it was the Newark Priory, an Augustinian abbey. Now, only the shell of the sanctuary remained.

Jessica wanted to walk along the bridge wall, and I helped her up. The wall wasn't high, but it left her on the precipice. If she fell on my side, I would catch her. The other side was steep and would have caused injury if she toppled over. 'Hold my hand, Dad,' she said. I was concerned; she was insistent.

Halfway across, I wanted her to step down. Of course, she didn't. The excitement and tension propelled her forward. I was glad when it was over, and I trembled as I lifted her down. I never forgot that moment. It has been seared into my memory. That wall at Ripley. In her own way, she was letting me know that she was a risk-taker. Like me.

Jessica wanted to touch the sky, to walk on the highest bridge (to her). In Ripley, I was by her side to hold her hand. But I wouldn't always be there, and it worried me. She just loved life. Ready to experiment. Jessica went charging full force into the future, eager to explore everything and taste everything. Borders were there to be crossed; boundaries didn't exist. She was shrewd and smart, sassy and bold when she needed to be, unafraid to push the envelope. And taking risks was part of the thrill of being alive.

I was worried about Jessica because I recognized myself in her. She had my DNA, my heart. I understood her like no one else. I wanted to raise my hands to catch her if she fell. I wanted to go before her, prepare the ground, find the cliffs she could tumble over, move any sharp stones in her path. From this point on, I took my phone everywhere, kept it near me when I slept. I told Jessica that she could phone me at any time, day or night, from anywhere and I would go to her.

\* \* \*

It was difficult for us, but hardest for Rachel, two years younger.

Jessica had grown accustomed to getting her way. As the only child, then the eldest, she knew she commanded her parents' undivided attention. As her little sister grew, it became difficult for that space and attention to be shared or for her to accept someone else alongside her. From Jessica's view of the world, there wasn't room for anyone else. I was hurt by the situation and spoke privately to her; I know she tried, but she couldn't contain her emotions. Rachel evolved her own way to deal with things but living with such tensions would grind her down. This was an extremely difficult time for Rachel, and for us.

* * *

Our campaigns dealt with adult themes and I wanted to shield Jessica from our troubled world. One of the most shocking stories I'd ever heard was about abandoned children inside China.

David Alton introduced me to Brian Woods and Kate Blewett from True Vision, in a room at the Norman Shaw building in Westminster. These investigative journalists had gone undercover in China at great personal risk. They filmed secretly in orphanages where unwanted female and disabled children were left to die, abandoned so that their parents could have another child. This was the result of China's One Child Policy, a brutal population control programme launched in 1979.

Their harrowing film *The Dying Rooms* has been viewed by an estimated global audience of 100 million, and former BBC chairman Lord Grade named it his greatest documentary of all time. It was impossible not to be moved; we lobbied the Chinese authorities and gave practical support for the charity set up by the filmmakers. Later, they interviewed me for their follow-up film *Return to the Dying Rooms*, broadcast in 1996 on Channel 4 TV.

I knew this documentary would upset Jessica, so I waited till she had gone up to bed before watching the film on the night it was broadcast.

When she returned from school the next day, she was furious.

'Dad! Why didn't you tell me you were on television about the children in China?'

Jessica's friends had seen her father on television. She quizzed me about the story and asked for our campaign materials.

'Promise me you will always tell me about what you're doing and never keep anything from me again,' she insisted.

Jessica got a buzz from the activities of a busy office. She wasn't content to sit in a corner and read a book. She wanted to be part of the action, and one of the team. If the bins were full, she'd empty them; she would sharpen the pencils; dust the books on the shelf; refill empty cups with tea or coffee and stamp the post at the end of the day. As she grew so did her responsibilities. She liked answering the phone. 'You want Mr Smith,' she would say, giving me one of her 'looks'. No one had briefed her on what to say or do, but she handled the calls with a confidence and professionalism beyond her age.

Kate, our brilliant fund-raiser, was unperturbed by her untidy desk and random forgetfulness. Jessica and I had dropped into the office one Saturday afternoon and she noticed a used plate tucked away on a shelf under Kate's desk. On the spur of the moment we came up with a cunning plan. We took the plate home, put it through the dishwasher and returned it on Sunday, replacing it exactly where it had been concealed. If Kate noticed that the plate had been tampered with, she said nothing. Each day when I returned home, Jessica asked me if Kate had discovered it. She hadn't.

Jessica was about twelve when she took charge of a class magazine and convinced about a dozen school chums to get involved. One weekend, we took all the contributions to Wonersh and she set about producing thirty copies of the first edition. Jessica was editor, designer and producer. She colour-coordinated the ten pages, set the layout and collated the magazine in a red ring binder. She'd figured out how to use the binding machine, a feat that had stumped me until that point.

We were in the car in south London when Jessica told me she wanted to take action against the blood sport of fox hunting and asked for help. 'I have to do something, Dad.' She didn't waste time. Her petition ran to four pages and was posted to Philip Hammond, our local MP, and she sent a press release to the local papers.

When the 4 December 1997 edition of the paper was pushed through our letterbox a few weeks later, I saw a photo of Jessica on the front page with the headline: 'Friend of Fox'.

I rushed it over to her. She shrugged nonchalantly, 'Ah, good.'

Apparently, the reporter followed up Jessica's press release, turned up at Fullbrook School and obtained special dispensation from the head teacher to interview and photograph Miss Smith. The paper contacted Mr Hammond's office, who said the MP would be writing 'a detailed reply to Jessica as soon as possible.'

\* \* \*

When she turned thirteen, I wrote these words in her birthday card: 'I know you want to fly, to soar high. And I want you to fly. But I want you to fly safe.'

As I watched my beautiful daughter turning from my adorable little girl into a tempestuous young teen, this question came to me: 'What can I give you for the journey . . . ?'

Those words stayed with me. They became my prayer for Jessica.

For her thirteenth birthday, Jessica had asked for money because she'd decided to buy a pair of 20-centimetre-high platform heels exactly like the ones worn by the Spice Girls. Eventually she hit the magic number of one hundred pounds. It was an astounding amount of money to be spent on a pair of 'Look at me' shoes. Everyone tried to talk her out of it, but she wouldn't budge. I'd been persuaded to take her to London on the weekend before her birthday to spend her bounty. We took the train to Waterloo and I caught the delight in her face.

'Last chance to change your mind Jessica.'

'No, Dad. This is what I want to do.'

I collapsed the resistance. I told her I was proud of her for sticking to her decision. I think it was the first time that I'd fully realized that this was more than just a fan's desire to mimic their favourite pop star. It was a fashion statement.

We walked from Covent Garden's tube station to 47-49 Neal Street. There it was: Buffalo, the only shop in London selling these shoes. Jessica had presence; without a hint of intimidation she checked out the colours and asked for a pair in black. She was the youngest person in this super-cool shop and I'm certain the only one accompanied by a parent.

'What do you think Dad?'

'Fabulous,' I replied.

She gave me that special look.

She walked confidently to the till. 'I'll take them,' and she counted out ten crisp £10 notes. They gave her 10p change.

She wore them out of the shop, of course. The platform heels were the latest craze and created a buzz as she strutted across the cobblestone square in Covent Garden. Everyone we passed stared at her. She took the attention she created in her stride. It was her way of saying 'Hello world. Here I am!'

She wore her Buffalos everywhere. My friend Wanno Haneveld's partner, Ton, owned a luxury boutique in Holland where he dressed Dutch celebrities for television shows and film premieres. Ton bolstered Jessica's confidence and encouraged her pursuit of style and fashion. He was the only adult whose first response was positive. 'This makes her who she is,' he said. I understood her better after listening to Ton. She was stylish and cool. Her Buffalo boots fitted her persona and affirmed her identity.

That February, Jessica invited every relative she knew to celebrate her thirteenth birthday. Her 'Family United' theme brought together our many cousins for the first time in a decade.

I'd taught Jessica a 12-bar blues riff and we played this with the family gathered around the piano. We started with Jessica on the treble and me playing the bass line. At some point, we switched. Jessica moved from right to left on the piano as she swapped with me, while I took up her part on the treble. All this without missing a beat. We were rewarded with rousing applause.

But the hit of the party was Jessica's Buffalo footwear. Everyone loved them. No one was surprised: after all, this was Jessica.

Jessica became intrigued by her family history. The fragments I could recall didn't satisfy her curiosity but only served to increase it. So, one evening we visited my mother and her husband, Clement Dameron, who had settled in sheltered accommodation about fifteen minutes away in Horsell.

It was fascinating to watch grandmother beside her granddaughter, who was attentive, notebook in hand, eyes widening as the story of a life was retold and tales of exploits of adventure and intrigue unfolded. I saw the admiration in my daughter's eyes and the emotion in my mother's face, as secrets locked in the past tumbled out, dragged into the light of a teenager's explorations into her history and identity. It was like entering a cave and following after a guide with a torchlight who led you deeper into the cavern.

Many of my mother's recollections had been known to me but eroded with the passage of time. I had a vague notion of an uncle who had been awarded the OBE for his medical work in Burma during World War II. I'd forgotten my mother's encounter with Mahatma Gandhi, when she'd been selected to garland the Indian leader during one of his legendary campaigns of civil disobedience. I was named after the song 'Danny Boy' but didn't know that her grandfather's fascination with Ireland's independence had sparked my mother's interest in India's struggle for freedom, and her passion for social justice. Neither did I fully comprehend her love of India, or the impact of her father's sudden death in Crickhowell, Wales, after he lost all his savings in his brother's failed get rich quick scheme.

My grandmother Effie had returned to India after this and established herself as a head teacher at several railway schools set up during the British Raj. She married again but the saga of Effie's third marriage was dramatic. Her husband disappeared one day from their home. On a trip to Calcutta, Effie stumbled on news in a chance encounter in the city's famed New Market. The scoundrel had secretly married his mistress while still wed to my grandmother. Effie learned that her husband and his new bride had set sail for England. Effie reported the news to her father, who contacted the British police. When the bigamist set foot on Southampton docks, the police were there waiting for him, with handcuffs.

It was too much for one evening – and on a school night. Despite her pleas for 'Five minutes more' we drove home, Jessica buzzing with ideas and fired up with more questions that I couldn't answer. 'Can we see Nanny tomorrow evening? There's so much I want to know. Please Dad.'

I didn't take much persuading. I was as intrigued as the young historian.

My mother must have been yearning to share her story, and the history of our family. Now her wish was granted. For Jessica, it was intoxicating. She was energized by every hour spent with her grandmother.

* * *

That year, Jessica considered options for her future career with flirtations in several directions. She took a GCSE course in law; aged 13, she was the youngest student enrolled at the Runnymede Adult Education Centre in Surrey. She'd learned by then how much lawyers earned. A friend arranged work experience at their law firm near the Royal Courts of Justice. We worked out a short cut from the Underground and I travelled the route with her before she started. Jessica loved the daily commute into the heart of the capital city. But the drama and theatrics of the courtroom didn't match the reality of the backroom operation with its grind of procedural requirements. She didn't take to it.

* * *

When I was growing up, music filled our home. My grandmother was a musician and I was expected to follow in the family tradition of playing the piano. But I hated to practice, while my grandmother threatened that I would come to no good if I neglected my daily musical exercises.

My mother played the popular songs of the day. I watched in admiration as her fingers whizzed over the keyboard of our upright rented piano. We regularly visited Braganza Musicals on Marquis Street. There was no other place in the city like it. The shop was famed for importing foreign (original) musical instruments and the latest sheet music. After picking out a new song, we'd take a taxi home and mum would set the sheet music up on the piano and run through the melody. We had a rosewood gramophone that could stack several 78rpm vinyl records at a time. Billie Holliday and Glenn Miller were favourites.

I was about 13 when Duke Ellington played a concert at the Grand Hotel on Chowringhee Road. I can still recall the excitement when the Duke strolled on stage, snapping his fingers to the beat. He appeared from the left and walked to the centre of the stage, bowed to his rapturous audience, then ambled over to where the song's composer Billy Strayhorn was seated at the piano. Ellington replaced Strayhorn. His hands hit the keyboard as the opening chords of 'Take the A Train' filled the auditorium. I was mesmerized by the hypnotic rhythm of those opening bars.

A few days earlier, I'd infiltrated the Grand Hotel and using stealth and guile, obtained autographs from Ellington, Johnny Hodges, Cat Anderson and other band members. It was both a dare and an intrigue, while the notion of failure never entered my mind. The encounter fired me up and set my life's direction for music and creative writing.

The turning point had been hearing Elvis for the first time. I'd discovered my 'own' music. Perhaps it was even more exciting because of the disapproval that erupted from adults. My grandmother was furious, my mother tolerant.

RCA Victor didn't have a licensing deal in India, so Elvis' records weren't available; however, a few sold at great cost on the black market. The only place to hear Elvis was on a juke box in Magnolia, a cafe in the New Market. I'd spend days thinking about which song to play before the ice melted in my fresh lime soda.

I was thrilled when a friend returned from London with an Elvis record for me. I ripped the packaging and stared at the extended play disc with four gospel songs. 'Precious Lord take my hand' had feeling, but it wasn't the hard driving 'Hound Dog' or the super cool 'Don't be Cruel'. I was disappointed. The song however had a message that would resonate decades later.

Jessica inherited my love of music. I lined up the musical trajectory for her to follow. I was her guide. Starting point: Elvis, of course. But as she grew, she strayed and swerved beyond the route I had selected. Still, she embraced all the musical genres with relish. She overturned the order in the same way I had done in my youth and charted her own musical journey, covering Destiny's Child, Fugees, Lauryn Hill and numerous rap, soul and R&B bands.

Music surrounded her from the moment she awoke. Finding Jessica was easy, just follow the music. If I entered the house and heard music, one thing was certain: Jessica was home. Jessica could listen to a song for the first time and predict the hits.

The Spice Girls captured her imagination with their mix of music and fashion. Their first album wore itself out in our car. Even my VW Passat reacted in fury and chewed up the cassette tape. I startled the office one day when I unexpectedly blurted out a lyric from one of their hits.

\* \* \*

Jessica loved pets and on our Saturday adventures we covered hundreds of miles to view different species of birds, wildlife, reptiles and various life forms from the animal kingdom. Inevitably, some of them travelled home with us. Jessica had stick insects, which she bred, and she sold the offspring. Almost unstoppable, she bought red-bellied newts and later Malaysian box turtles; at the time of purchase each one would fit into the palm of my hand.

Jessica volunteered after school every Friday at the Rosemount Veterinary Centre in West Byfleet. When I picked her up after the clinic closed, she would tell me about the pets she'd dealt with. One of the vets spotted her enthusiasm and would explain the problem with the animal or bird he was dealing with. Even if it was a complex procedure, he still went through the details with his attentive volunteer. She absorbed it all, and the experience energized her. Whenever a wounded bird or animal required special attention, she provided an after-care service. Thoughtfully, Jessica involved Joan in her scheme and assigned her the task of cleaner. She was literally taking her work home with her. Her bedroom (in the loft) was turned into a wildlife sanctuary. Wounded and recuperating birds perched around her room. At one point, she had four birds that were receiving TLC. I captured a series of photographs as Jessica released the birds she'd help to recover into a bright clear blue sky.

And it wasn't just wounded birds that she brought home.

About 6.00am one Monday morning, our bedroom door was flung open and 14-year old Jessica stumbled in, barely awake. She was in her school uniform but had obviously dressed in a rush. She mumbled a garbled message. 'Early . . . don't worry . . . got lunch . . . school . . . bye.'

The next sound was the front door slamming.

Joan and I were mystified. What had just happened? I shuffled to the bedroom window which overlooked the street but couldn't spot Jessica. When she returned from school, she withdrew to her room and kept to herself for the rest of the day. It was unlike her. When the same thing happened the next day, we were determined to solve the mystery. Did she have a secret boyfriend? Was she bunking off school?

On the third morning, I was ready. I pulled on some clothes and rushed to my car which was parked on the driveway. I drove around the streets near our house, past the school, the railway station, her friend's house. Nothing.

The mystery was revealed on the fourth day.

A girl from her class had run away from home. Jessica had hidden her, and she had lived secretly in our house for the past four days. Jessica was leaving early to sneak the girl out of our home and onto the next safe house.

We had no option but to contact the police and social services – against Jessica's wishes. The runaway stayed with us for a further few days until we drove her to a foster home. Jessica surveyed the property, providing support and reassurance to her friend.

Jessica guarded her private world from prying parents. We were concerned that she'd become entangled in situations that could put her at risk. Sometimes we only found out what was happening when we broke the rules.

One day – not for the first time – I was eavesdropping on her private conversation with a friend. Jessica listened to her friend's troubles and offered advice and encouragement. I was proud of how she handled herself. I thought I had got away with it and reported to Joan in the kitchen. I turned around. Jessica was standing there. She was furious and had a right to be. I apologized but her look told me that she knew I couldn't be trusted not to do it again.

Jessica volunteered at another local animal rescue centre. It was struggling financially so she worked on a marketing plan and recruited me to meet the owner. She outlined practical suggestions of how it could overcome its problems. Later, she kept notes about the pets' ill-treatment and other irregularities, including her suspicion that the owner slept on the premises, apparently illegally. But before she could turn over her raw intelligence to the authorities, she needed proof that he never left the centre at night. Then she hit on an idea: a stake-out.

I picked her up one Friday night after finishing her shift at the centre. We raced home, had dinner, and packed our detective kit: notebook, pen, torch, snacks, drinks. Later that evening we cruised past the centre. She'd figured out where we could park with a clear sight of the front entrance of the centre. She was right. The lights were on. It was 9pm.

The surveillance by the amateur detective with her accomplice and getaway driver lasted several hours. Around 11.30pm the lights at the centre went out. The owner's car was in the drive. The young sleuth took notes and kept a file of dates of irregularities with the intention of compiling a report for the authorities. On other nights we would drive by after 10:30pm and spot lights from our surveillance hide-out. Since Jessica had school the following day, and I had a job, we'd pack up. Eventually, she handed in her notice. I was relieved, but the situation troubled her. We'd drive past at night to find the lights on. Not long afterwards, the place shut down.

One Saturday morning, Jessica and I set off for London on one of our escapades. This time we travelled by train; our destination: a shop on the Kings Road in Chelsea.

Soon after the train pulled out of Weybridge Station, Jessica nudged me. I followed her gaze. Between two seats inside the British Rail compartment was . . . a baby bat. She instinctively knew how to deal with the situation. Jessica caught the bat, delicately wrapped it in my handkerchief and made space in my cloth carry-bag for the tiny mammal which measured a few inches in length. I was given strict instructions on how to hold the bag so it wouldn't be hurt. We cut short our plans in London and returned home with the bat. She named it Waterloo, but it was nick-named 'Batty'.

Waterloo was kept in a faunarium, a plastic tank for keeping pets, for a few weeks, and kept warm during his recuperation by a heat-pad. Jessica fed the bat by hand with a drip until it was ready for the outside world. For several years afterwards, Batty could be seen circling our home on dusky nights.

* * *

We had known Craig and Janet Rickards when they were a courting couple in Cobham and when we moved to New Haw, we were pleased to learn they lived about half a mile away. Craig had practical skills and rebuilt their bungalow himself to allow for their growing family. As someone who couldn't hang a picture on the wall, I respected his abilities, but admired his musical talent more. I'd harboured dreams of getting lessons from him in blues/jazz piano, but it was Jessica and Rachel who beat me to it.

The Rickards attended All Saints Church in Woking and Joan and Jessica joined them. Rachel was already there. She spent more time at the Rickards house than with us. Rachel was adamant that the Rickards were the gold standard for home life. If something questionable happened in our house, Rachel would scold us: 'The Rickards would never allow that in their home!'

In early autumn, All Saints announced a six-week instructional course in baptism, and 14-year old Jessica decided to investigate. I drove her down for the initial class and picked her up an hour later.

'How was it?'

'Interesting,' she replied.

We talked about baptism on the ten-minute journey to the church the following week. She was the only teenager in the group and mostly on her own.

One evening towards the end of the programme, I asked her, 'How are you feeling about the course?'

'It's OK,' she replied.

Perhaps she thought I was trying to influence her. She looked directly at me. 'Dad, don't expect me to get baptized just because you want me to.'

'I only wanted to know how it was going,' I replied.

'It's going OK. But don't be disappointed if I don't go through with it. I haven't decided.'

No one could make Jessica do anything she didn't want to do.

She completed the course. She made the decision herself. She got baptized.

The ceremony was a formal high Church of England service attended by the bishop of the diocese. The other girls wore first-communion dresses. Jessica wore black. It was her distinctive goth-look. She asked Janet and Craig Rickards to stand as her references.

Some years later, Jessica talked about her faith journey when we had lunch at a local restaurant. It was clear to me that this foundation would remain a part of her life.

But there were challenges.

She pushed the limits, defied our rights as her parents to curb her choices or restrict her movements. 'What do you know? Why should I listen to you?' was a gauntlet hurled at us. Arguments ensued, rages followed, and we never knew when things would erupt. She knew there were rules. It's just that the rules didn't apply to her.

I heard this recently, and it reminded me of Jessica's teenage years: Orchids are difficult to look after but beautiful when they flower.

\* \* \*

In the nineties, we launched a campaign with Fr Shay Cullen in the Philippines to lobby the UK government to prosecute British sex tourists who exploited children overseas. After obstacles and excuses, the government agreed legislation in 1996 that proved one thing: campaigning works. We already supported Fr Shay's work in Olongapo City but wanted another small charitable project. On a visit to India, a friend urged me to meet someone in Mumbai. It was to be an unforgettable experience.

Reverend Devaraj led me into the back streets of Mumbai's notorious red-light district. The brothel owners, girls and women who'd been tricked or forced into the sex industry trusted him and I got to hear their stories. Later that night, he led me on a hunt to meet a 14-year old girl called Asha. Her mother was a prostitute but had died, leaving Asha to look after her younger sister and brother. Her mother's boyfriend, a taxi driver, was threatening to sell Asha to a brothel for about 50,000 rupees (about six hundred pounds). Eventually, we tracked her to a local school where she had taken shelter for the night. She was like a hidden treasure amidst the soiled sordid torment of this slave pit. I asked if she could be rescued.

'Yes, it's possible,' Devaraj told me.

'What do we have to do?'

He said we needed a house outside the city.

I was haunted by the image of this beautiful young girl whose life was about to be ruined. The safe house would cost over £30,000. It was a huge amount of money. I decided we had to get the money and rescue Asha before the door of another house opened and her life was lost forever. It was a race against time.

There was resistance to this project in the office, but I was determined to push through. I took leaflets home, and everyone pitched in. I signed hundreds of letters and we posted them with a hope and a prayer that people would respond.

Our supporters were generous. One of the larger gifts came from Olivia and George Harrison. Steve Brown gave us the money from Billy Connolly's benefit concert in London. We reached our target. Asha was rescued. The (first) Jubilee Home cost about £50,000. Steve became a good friend and followed the progress of the Jubilee Home. With Billy's concert money, we built a second home. More children were rescued.

When I raised the difficulty of paying for the operating costs of both Jubilee Homes, Steve invented Tickety-Boo Tea to sell in UK supermarkets with the profits given to us for the Jubilee Homes. It was an inspired idea and the excitement increased after Steve decided to launch it on a tea clipper on the Thames in October 1999. When the media heard that Billy would be on board for the cruise, everyone wanted a ticket to sail.

Jessica followed the project in India after my first visit. She was enthralled by the rescue of a young girl like her and wanted to meet Asha. When she heard about the launch of Tickety-Boo Tea, she was determined it was one party she wasn't going to miss. She was 14 but took a day off school (with our approval) and joined me for my best day at the office.

Jessica was excited. But cool. She looked great in her Tickety-Boo t-shirt. We were one of the first on board, followed by Billy and Steve.

Billy was great. When I introduced my daughter, he said, 'Jessica! What a lovely name. Nice to meet you.'

One of the photographers captured Billy shaking hands with Jessica, but she shrieked when she saw the photos.

'Dad, don't show this picture to anyone.'

Later, she agreed we could publish other pictures we'd taken together.

The clipper set off from Tower Bridge and sailed to Greenwich and back again. Billy talked to everyone about Tickety-Boo Tea and the Jubilee Homes and the coverage was fantastic. ITV did a live link for their midday news. During a quick coffee break, Jessica got talking with Billy about music.

'My Dad's a big Elvis fan,' she told Billy.

'I like Elvis,' he replied, 'particularly that Comeback Special TV concert in 1968.'

On the way home that night, we stopped at a Tesco Superstore. Although we expected it to be on the shelf, it was still a shock to see Tickety-Boo Tea alongside such familiar brands as PG Tips and Typhoo. The day had been a success, and everyone left on a high. The idea that everyone who bought Tickety-Boo Tea contributed to the running costs of the Jubilee Homes was fantastic. Even I became a tea drinker. But I was inspired by something that happened before the launch.

At Tower Bridge, just before we approached the clipper, Jessica linked her arm in mine. She looked at me and said, 'I want to work with you, Dad. I want to be like you. I want to do the same things you do.'

She hugged me. It was an enduring and cherished moment between father and daughter that lives on in my memory.

CHAPTER 4

# Fashionista

*2000 – 2004*

Jessica signed on as a recruit with the Army Cadets Force when she was about 13 and I drove her to Chobham every week where the country's largest youth voluntary programme had barracks. At first, we suspected this new-found diversion might have been a pretext to meet local boys who were part of the contingent. I wondered how long the fad would last.

But I'd misjudged her. The Chobham barracks became a regular destination over the next two years. It was ironic. This teen rebel who pushed against home rules was captured by the rugged programme, and the discipline of the Surrey detachment's activities had arrested her imagination. In August 1999, aged 15, she enrolled in a two-week summer training course. This included a three-day outdoor survival exercise on the Yorkshire Moors.

I picked her up on Sunday afternoon after the endurance exercise. She looked stronger, resilient, a maturity that was discernible in the way she moved.

Later, we learned how gruelling and intense the drill had been. She (and her detachment – but operating as individuals) had to survive outdoors for three days without even a tent, each drawing on their own skills, resources and daring. It was tough, and even some of the boys on the course had given up. In a disarming way, she told me, 'That was the hardest thing I've ever done.'

That summer, we gathered one Sunday morning at the Army Training Regiment in Deepcut Surrey for their annual graduation parade. Jessica, in full uniform, marched with her detachment. I felt a surge of pride when her name was called: 'Cadet Jessica Smith.' She strode forward, took the salute, marched back, and received our applause. It was well deserved.

Eventually, she ended her involvement but kept in touch with others in her brigade. A few years later, Jessica turned up unexpectedly at our office in Wonersh with a boy dressed in full army uniform. I hardly recognized him. He had been one of the teenagers from the Chobham barracks. After graduating, he joined the army and his first posting was to Afghanistan. Before leaving for the war zone, he'd called on Jessica and she'd driven him over to say goodbye to me. It took a few minutes for the news to sink in. He'd been in the back of my car when I dropped everyone home after cadets, and his home in Horsell had been a regular route for 'Dad's Taxi'. Even though he wore the khaki uniform of a soldier in the British army, to me he looked like a kid. Now, within hours, he'd fly over 3,500miles to Afghanistan, and join others who put their life at risk in a conflict that had already claimed countless casualties on all sides.

I am not a pacifist, but the reality of war hit home in a new way that day.

* * *

Jessica could read people and had a natural understanding of situations. In the office, she never used her position of being 'the boss's daughter' to show off or advance her ideas. Neither did she contradict or argue with me, though that was taken for granted when we were alone.

Sometimes, after work, we'd go out for dinner. We'd guess who the others were in the restaurant; spies passing coded messages, having a clandestine rendezvous; and we would try to eavesdrop on conversations.

Jessica came to work with me over the school holidays and made friends with the team. Emily Murray-Swain, a former actress who had a role in Michael Caine's movie *Shiner*, took her to the Greenbelt music festival. In the office, she developed a friendship with Mark Rowland, who eventually became our assistant director. Jessica was convinced he was an important asset. 'He's good for Jubilee.'

We hired Mark in 1999 to work on the campaign for James Mawdsley, jailed in Burma after a peaceful protest. David Alton launched our campaign on a ship that was docked near Lambeth Bridge. Jessica's role was to welcome guests and the media; with all on board, we sailed down the Thames for a half hour cruise. A television reporter recognized Jessica from the launch of Tickety-Boo Tea and questioned why this 15-year old teenager was campaigning. Jessica was undaunted and rehearsed her response with me.

After we returned to dry land, David Alton invited us for a meal. We stopped first at a pub near Covent Garden and were joined by Fr Michael Seed and an actor named Tim. Jessica was an enthusiastic part of the evening. The next day, she became animated when she learned that Tim was the son of Edward Woodward.

'Whaaaat? That's amazing! Edward Woodward is the most wonderful actor. He inspired me. I wanted to become an actress after seeing him. I can't believe I was talking to his son.'

She talked about this encounter for days. I didn't know she'd seen Edward Woodward perform. She kept her life private and shared things on her own terms. She had several rooms in her metaphysical house. Some doors were locked. Only she had a key. Only she could let you in.

Jessica was agitated over James Mawdsley's imprisonment.

'Do you really think he'll be jailed for seventeen years?' she asked me on the drive to work one day.

'I don't know. Maybe,' I replied.

'But they can't do that, can they?' She was outraged.

In October 2000, the shock news took us by surprise: the Burmese government released James. Days later, we joined his family at the airport to welcome him. James' return was prominently reported, and our involvement was featured in the coverage.

When Jessica learned that James' book about his experiences was set for release in September 2001, her response was, 'Cool.' She held onto the invitation for the book launch when it arrived, and left the event clutching an autographed copy of *The Heart Must Break*.

Meeting James was important to her. She respected his great commitment, but even though her role had been minimal in comparison, she wasn't diminished by it. She had a part to play. And she played it.

* * *

We encouraged our children to pursue their dreams and their interests. Rachel's aspiration was to be a mother and establish a home of her own. Luke would turn his enthusiasm for computer games into a career. For Jessica, it was fashion. She had a strong sense of style and design. Her best friend Charlotte Saunders remembered her this way: 'You were cool Jessica. And you always knew what was cool.' Jessica's textile teacher at Fullbrook School declared that she had the best eye for design she'd seen in someone so young, and her creative talents led her naturally to fashion.

Jessica set her sights high. She applied for a place at the London College of Fashion (LCF) on Oxford Street in London. LCF is linked to the University of Arts London and was the only British college, at the time, to specialize in fashion education, research and consultancy. It ranked among the best in the world and reportedly had 200 applicants for every place. I encouraged her, but was secretly worried that it would dent her self-confidence if she couldn't get in.

Her interview at LCF was set for April. I can remember everything about the day. The way she looked – older than her sixteen years. She stood on the patio for a photograph in the early morning sunlight. Her hair was pinned back, her make-up discreet. A cool black coat dress with a silver belt had been chosen from the dozens in her wardrobe. Realizing appearance would be important and knowing our budget was limited, Joan and Jessica had headed to TK Maxx a week earlier. They scoured the rails till they found exactly the right garment with a bargain basement price tag. Jessica customized it from her many accessories. She wasn't flashy but carried herself with an aura of confidence that conveyed style and elegance.

The LCF campus is near London's Oxford Street. We took the train to Waterloo and the tube to Bond Street. She was excited, but nervous. The hall was packed with prospective students. We checked her name on the list. Jessica Smith: afternoon interview. With hours to spare, we walked to Selfridges to pick out a dress for her end of year prom. She went through their extensive collection and selected a scarlet full-length ball gown. She looked sensational.

We returned to LCF after lunch. She looked professional, with an impressive portfolio of work. But interviews are random, and with so many young hopefuls, I couldn't predict how it would go. Finally, her name was called. She disappeared into an inner chamber and returned about forty minutes later. She glanced at me and I decoded her look. I want to leave. Now! We walked silently towards the exit.

As we stepped out of the building, she told me, 'They didn't like me Dad . I'm not going to get in.' I recognized the stress in her voice. We reached Oxford Street in a few strides and headed for the underground. She walked in silence, looking straight ahead, disappointment scrawled across her face, like graffiti scratched on a wall.

She had been seated outside the interview room and listened to the students before her; she thought this would give her an edge. But when it was her turn, the examiners' questions surprised her.

'They didn't ask me any of the questions they'd asked the others. Everything was different.'

I probed deeper.

'They wanted to know my favourite designers. What I wanted to do. My interests. If I made my own clothes. If anyone in my family was in the fashion industry. It wasn't an interview but more like a conversation.'

I developed a growing conviction that her sense of style and the design work she presented had set her aside from the others. I could tell she was getting a little more hopeful. 'Your presence made an impact when you walked through the door. They knew you were different. They recognized that flair, that style, in you.'

'Do you really think I could have got through, Dad?'

'I do, Jessica,' I said, reminding her about the excellent portfolio of work she'd taken with her. Her confidence grew as we talked on the journey home, and she started to relax. She wasn't sure, but this time she was willing to trust my judgement.

A few months later, the answer arrived in a crisp white envelope emblazoned with the distinctive LCF logo. The letter was brilliant. It was an unqualified offer. They didn't just want her. LCF were waving her in.

\* \* \*

On a late sunny afternoon on 9 May 2001, a glossy and sparkling white limousine pulled up outside our house.

Jessica had booked the car for the major social event of the year: the school prom. Jessica and her friends, all in dazzling gowns, climbed into the limo, and took off on a tour of local Surrey sights, before the luxury vehicle delivered their youthful passengers to the school gates.

Joan and I waved the girls goodbye and walked to Fullbrook School, about half a mile away. Parents, relatives and friends had already started to gather and eager family members lined the street outside the school entrance. We'd been waiting for a while when the first vehicle pulled up. It was a glistening white limousine. The door opened and Jessica stepped out. She looked stunning (an unbiased opinion), like a glamorous movie star at a film premiere. Her long black hair was styled off her shoulders and the scarlet ball gown from Selfridges was the perfect choice.

People on both sides of the street yelled her name. Jessica! Jessica! I called out as well. Eventually she heard me amidst the noise and bustle and came over. I raised my camera and tried to shoot off some photographs. But I was being jostled and she was distracted as people continued to call her name. Still, earlier that afternoon, she had posed for my camera in the garden. This way. That way. Look up. Look down. Turn left. No, not that much. And so it went. Finally, she got frustrated. 'Enough, Dad, enough photos.'

Six years later, it would be one of these photographs that newspapers used in their reports about her passing, and the image is shown on the back cover of this book.

\* \* \*

Five months later, in early September, we returned to London to complete the process of registration on her first day at LCF.

Jessica was excited but kept her sense of cool. It took a few hours as we queued at various points, and she filled in all the forms. She carried that feeling of pride and accomplishment, but every now and again I glimpsed the little girl in her, caught up in the thrill and excitement of the moment. Her eyes would light up. She'd look at me and smile, the most wonderful smile. It made me so happy.

With registration completed, we rushed to Oxford Street and took a taxi to Notting Hill. Jessica planned to get her hair braided and was late for an appointment with a West London stylist. The taxi driver was listening to the radio and near Portobello Road, he turned to us in the back of his cab: 'Did you hear that? A plane crashed into the World Trade Center in New York.'

The cabbie turned up the volume. It didn't make much sense. We set off for a nearby shop. Jessica wanted to buy snacks and a drink because the braiding would take a few hours. We headed down Portobello Road in the direction of the hair saloon when someone yelled out that a second plane had crashed into a building in New York. The street erupted, as people shouted across the road to each other. Doors were flung open, and people stood in the street, speculating wildly. One of the street hawkers gestured to us, 'It's like the end of the world.'

For an instant flash, it was as though the secular prophecy from the media guru Marshall McLuhan had come true. We belonged in a global village. A lone rider had brought bad news from a far country. Raiders had torched their compound. We had a shared yet unknown enemy. And just momentarily we felt this connection, stranger to stranger, bound by our collective humanity and united by a common purpose.

Whenever '9/11' was mentioned, Jessica would look at me and catch my eye. No words were needed. It became a memory of an unforgettable event.

At the end of her first year, LCF students organized a fashion show at a theatre off Oxford Street. Jessica was one of the models on the catwalk, in a professional and dazzling event. We saw her briefly afterwards, one of many proud parents huddled around their children. On our way out, a group of girls approached us. One said, 'Are you Jessica's parents?'

We nodded, hesitantly. What was it? Did she owe money? Had she been in trouble?

The girl's eyes lit up. 'Jessica is amazing. She worked so hard on this event. You should be very proud.'

We returned home delighted with this affirmation. Jessica wasn't boastful, and this was a rare glimpse into her world at LCF.

Jessica's two years at the UK's top fashion college were a triumph. She relished the opportunity that LCF presented and loved the adventure of being in London. It delivered the independence that she coveted. It also saw her rise to the challenge of a competitive environment and produce assignments to a deadline. She enjoyed the experience and it paid off with top marks and the approval of her fellow students. It was clear that her future lay in fashion. After graduating successfully from the London College of Fashion in 2003, she enrolled at Manchester's Metropolitan University to study for a degree in Fashion Buying.

* * *

When our children were teenagers, and the subject of family holidays came up, there were groans. Everyone wanted to do something different, and in recent years the intensity of five people being cooped up together and forced to enjoy themselves had caused arguments and upsets.

Joan suggested that instead of a group holiday, we should take each child away, one at a time. It was a genius idea. In August 2003, Luke and I spent ten days in America. We stopped in Washington to meet with Ann Buwalda and the Jubilee Campaign US team and then headed to Memphis. Yes, our first stop was Graceland, the house Elvis bought for his mother, now one of the most visited private homes in the world. Interestingly, many of the visitors were parents with children, just like us.

Five months later, in January 2004, it was my turn again. Jessica and I headed out to India. Our first stop was Mumbai.

The mission to rescue one girl, Asha, had led to over a hundred at-risk children starting a new life in the Jubilee Homes. Furthermore, Reverend Devaraj had become a friend. He had a father's heart and expressed a genuine affection for each child who came his way, including my own children.

In Mumbai, Jessica and Asha developed a rapport. They'd discovered their birthdays were close: Asha's was on 26 February, Jessica's a day later. I'd always telephoned Asha on her birthday. It became understood that when I couldn't make that call, Jessica would take my place. Asha indulged Jessica's passion for shopping and the girls spent hours amidst the street vendors and shops of Colaba.

I'd chosen dates in January that coincided with Ann Buwalda's visit, to introduce a group of American congressmen to the project. Ann was leading the party so there wouldn't be much for me to do. The US delegation had stopped first in Pakistan and were due to arrive in Mumbai on an early evening flight from Islamabad. Devaraj had a prearranged meeting so asked me to step in and welcome the congressmen.

'Of course,' I said. It was my only assignment.

Devaraj organized a car and driver from Bombay Teen Challenge (BTC) that took us to the airport terminal. I hadn't bothered with any of the practical details of the trip since Ann was in charge. It felt good to be freed from responsibilities. Visitors aren't allowed inside the airport, so we stood on the pavement outside the terminal building. The sun was setting but it was still warm, eased by the occasional light breeze. Jessica's job was a look-out for Ann.

I heard the familiar ring tone of my Nokia 6310. It was Devaraj. 'I've just had a message from Ann. She's not on the plane. There's a problem with her visa. She's stuck at Delhi Airport.'

'Whaaat?'

'You'll have to take charge of the group.'

I had relied completely on Ann, so didn't have any

details about the congressmen's visit. Congressmen? I didn't even know their names, or how many were expected. Devaraj told me that there was a separate vehicle to transport the Americans from the airport to their hotel. Where was it?

Jessica took the news calmly. It was time for the 'Smith father & daughter' team to swing into gear.

We located the van assigned to the delegation, and soon after spotted about ten people, including congressmen, their aides and Indian church leaders. Porters and passers-by swelled the group into a small convoy, as we directed the procession towards the vehicle parked nearby. I was starting to feel the heat. Was it the weather or the stress? I hoped the vehicle's air-conditioning worked. The porters from the terminal jostled with unofficial coolies, while additional volunteers surged forward. It seemed everyone was shouting out suggestions, trying to get through the gawkers hanging on.

'Who is it?' someone asked me. 'Anyone famous? Hollywood stars?'

I ignored the question. Our main priority was to keep our eyes on the guests' luggage, to ensure nothing went 'walkabout'.

The congressmen identified their suitcases and boarded the van. A quick glance at the bus convinced me that we had to get a replacement for the drive to the Jubilee Homes the following day. At this point, the priority was to make sure that the vehicle transported everyone to the hotel in Nariman Point, a drive that could take anything from 45 minutes to four hours, depending on traffic.

With the congressmen on board and every seat taken, the only option was to load their luggage onto the roof of the van. On the street, the porters at the front of the van passed the first suitcase to another porter perched on top of the vehicle. Another porter climbed on the top of the bus and the suitcases were passed along to spread the weight evenly. A smart plan. We kept a close eye on the suitcases and assured the congressmen that their luggage had only one destination: on top of the bus they sat in.

The pavement and street were teeming with people. Everyone wanted to help. It seemed there were two to three people jostling each other in an attempt to get a single suitcase up top. The official porters were annoyed, while cries of 'Baksheesh,' rang out. The assembly line operated smoothly. Everything was working. Inside, bottled water was passed around as the air-conditioning started to kick in.

But why was it taking so long? How much luggage were these Americans travelling with?

Jessica and I decided to investigate. We'd focussed so hard on tracking the suitcases to make sure nothing disappeared amidst the melee that we hadn't noticed the activity at the top of the bus. We looked at each other in astonishment. There was an assembly line, but not one we had ordered.

It took a minute to grasp what was happening. The luggage was being loaded at the front of the bus then passed along to spread the load. A helpful porter at the back of the bus unloaded the last suitcase and passed it to someone else on the ground. It was then carried back to the assembly point at the front in a never-ending cycle. It was slapstick comedy straight out of a Laurel and Hardy movie.

With everyone shouting and barking out orders, it was hard to be heard. At some point, Devaraj returned, and together we prevailed. Finally, all the luggage was loaded, and it was time to hit the road. The van was full but Devaraj squeezed in and led the charge of the Americans to the hotel. Jessica and I headed for the BTC car.

'That was crazy!' Jessica said, her eyes sparkling. We couldn't stop laughing as we replayed the scene.

We arrived at the hotel in Nariman Point a few minutes before the guests and stumbled into the latest plot twist. There were no rooms available. The hotel staff were in a tizz. Who made the booking? In what name? When was it made? I couldn't answer any of the questions. The visitors arrived and sat in the hotel lobby. Suddenly – a light bulb moment. The booking was in the hotel next door. We were in the wrong place. Everyone hauled themselves up and walked the short distance to the adjourning building through a corridor that connected both hotels. Here, we were greeted by a smiling receptionist, 'Welcome. We've been waiting for you.'

It had been a long day. The group crashed out on the leather sofas in the lobby as the hotel registration got started.

I became aware that Jessica was going around the room with a pen and notebook. Eventually she reached one of the congressmen's aides, who'd been sitting with me.

'What are you doing, Jessica?'

'Everyone looked tired and thirsty, so I thought I'd order drinks for them. I was taking orders.'

It may have been an obvious thing to do but no one else had thought of it. I could have hugged her, but I knew that she'd be embarrassed if I'd dared to make such a move. She'd seen a problem and worked out a solution. And made a lot of friends.

It had been a rocky start but the next morning everyone looked refreshed. Overnight, two new vehicles had been booked and the journey to the Jubilee Homes passed without incident.

The Jubilee Homes were the tallest buildings in the area. They stood out on the horizon amidst an idyllic rural countryside, where everything looked fresh and green, so different from the urbanized teeming city of Mumbai. Devaraj and his team had done an amazing job. The visitors loved the work and were touched by the children they met: at the time, over fifty girls had been rescued and found new life at the Jubilee Homes.

Every time I saw Jessica, she was arm in arm with the Jubilee girls or cradling a child in her arms. In the group picture with the congressmen, she's shown feeding a youngster.

When we were in Mumbai, Asha had told us the story of Priya, a girl living on the streets near Victoria Terminus, the city's main railway station. Asha learned that an old man was abusing this young child. Asha wanted to hit him. She talked to Reverend Devaraj and Priya was rescued.

Jessica told me, 'After we arrived at the Jubilee Homes, I left the main hall and headed for the door when I bumped into a girl. We both laughed. I told her my name. "What's your name?" I asked her.'

Jessica's eyes were bright with wonder, 'Guess who it was?' She answered her own question: 'Priya.'

'I asked Priya what her plans were,' Jessica continued. 'She told me she wanted to work in the fashion industry. She was the first person I met.'

Jessica loved her time at the Jubilee Homes. Like everyone else, she was sad when it was time to leave.

'Jessica!' the girls called out her name. Many hugged her. 'Come back and visit us.'

'I will come back,' Jessica replied. In the vehicle, she said, 'Dad, I want to come back and work here. Can I?'

We agreed to talk about it later.

The next few days were busy as the congressmen learned more about Devaraj's work. We separated into smaller groups to ease the logistics. One evening we visited the shelter that we'd help to start four years earlier. It was in the heart of the sex industry and home to about forty children, but it also served as an immediate sanctuary if a child was in danger.

Devaraj told us that they'd rescued an abandoned boy named Prem. The child was desperately ill, possibly with suspected HIV; even the hospital wouldn't let him stay.

They advised Devaraj to keep Prem warm, so the boy was in a cot in a corner near the shelter's entrance. The entire body of the child was wrapped in a blanket: only his eyes and mouth were visible beneath a woollen cap. It seemed clear to me he was near death. I glanced at him, said a silent prayer but couldn't stay. I walked on to meet the other children.

Jessica went straight to Prem's cot. She huddled over him, stroking his frail body, whispering to him. She never left his side for the few hours of our visit. It was my enduring memory of our visit to the shelter.

The congressmen's trip had been a smash hit. On their final day, we met at the famous Taj Hotel before they set off for some last-minute shopping. They had an evening flight and it was agreed that we'd return to the Taj at three o'clock. Hopefully, we'd avoid the traffic jams and get everyone to the airport in time for their flight back.

Jessica wanted to explore the city on her own, and to see a snake charmer she'd spotted. I was uneasy but we agreed terms: don't wander down side streets; stick to the main shops; finally, be back before three.

Devaraj and I sat in the luxury of the Taj's air-conditioned lobby. He told me that Ann had been stuck inside Delhi Airport for three days ('I was on first name terms with the rats in the airport lounges,' she said later.). Dev hit the phone while I made notes in my journal. Gradually, the excited but weary tourists started to assemble near the Taj's entrance. By 2:50pm, the cars were lined up ready for the jaunt to the airport. Trent Franks, the politician from Arizona, told me he would never forget this trip. 'I'm truly inspired,' he said. Congressman Joseph Pitts nodded. 'This has been unforgettable.'

Devaraj called for a group photograph. One of the congressmen's aides asked me, 'Where's Jessica?'

For the last ten minutes, I'd been scouring the Taj. Nothing. I'd already decided that I wouldn't travel to the airport without her. I was focussed on how I was going to track her down. Before I could answer, I heard someone shout out, 'Jessica! We're taking a photo. It wouldn't be the same without you.'

Everyone laughed.

I looked at my watch. 3pm. Exactly.

'Sorry Dad.'

'What happened Jessica? I was so worried.'

On the drive to the airport, she told me the story.

She'd snapped a photograph of the snake charmer, and was strolling by the Gateway of India, the monument that overlooked the Arabian Sea built in 1911 to commemorate the visit of King George V and Queen Mary. Jessica was enjoying the waterfront view on the way back to the rendezvous when a teenager with a baby approached her. The girl looked exhausted. She told Jessica, 'I'm not asking you for money. Just buy some food for my baby. I'll take you to the shop. Pay the money yourself directly to the shopkeeper. After that, you can give it to me.'

'I had to do it Dad,' Jessica said.

Later, I told Devaraj the story. 'The girl was genuine. She didn't want the money herself,' I repeated the story. 'Jessica knew she was running a risk but had to help.' It hadn't escaped her attention that the girl was possibly even the same age, yet living a different life because of an accident of geography.

Devaraj smiled wryly. He recognized the likely scam. 'There's only one tin of food and lots of people pay for the same tin.'

We left Mumbai weary but inspired and continued on our journey to Calcutta and Delhi. When my two closest friends, Wanno Haneveld and Savitri 'Roley' Horowitz, had heard that Jessica was visiting India for the first time, they decided to join us to make this a memorable trip for my daughter.

My Dutch 'brother' Wanno had flown from Turkey. After his partner, Ton, closed his fashion business in Holland, they had moved to the coastal town of Bodrum. Roley was born in India, and spent her formative years in Japan, travelled the world with the airlines, but finally settled in Jerusalem and established herself as a leading tour guide. Amongst some of her clients are three former prime ministers of Australia, the current prime minister of India, journalists, diplomats and pilgrims of all faiths.

Jessica and I met Roley in Calcutta. We were immediately thrust into our first adventure. Roley wanted to trace one of her relatives who'd fallen on hard times, and she had a sketchy notion that her aunt was in a home for destitute women. Roley's relative had been a volunteer but succumbed to some inner turmoil and was unable to care for herself. After driving for hours into the countryside, we reached the shelter. The elderly woman lay in a darkened room but roused at Roley's cheerful smile. It was an emotional reunion, even for us who were passengers.

More escapades ensued. The next day, Roley led us to the High Court, the oldest in India, established in 1862. The High Court was on the Esplanade, once one of the finest streets in the city. Roley approached it from the side, through the crowded, cramped back streets and alleys, swamped by dirt and rubbish.

Roley led the way, Jessica followed, and I brought up the rear. The passages at times were so narrow that only single file traffic was permissible, as the sounds and smells of the city smacked our senses. Clerks crouched over antique typewriters, hammering out court summons and documents, some being translated and transcribed. Others were yelling out dictation to typists whose fingers flew at speed across the keyboard. A thicket of market stalls sold food and fabric, with bargains and baiting shouted out by vendors and clients. All this amidst the flight of crows, pigeons, parrots and other birds that swooped through the throng at the slightest hope of a snack before lunchtime. Dogs and cats roamed wild, while a cow stopped traffic from both sides; an anonymous oblivious Calcuttian relieved himself against a wall. The street widened but the congestion remained: a street labourer dripped sweat, struggling through the melee under the burden of his goods; a coconut-wallah cracked open one of the coolest healthiest drink on the thoroughfare.

Jessica was energized by these extraordinary few minutes, far removed from any tourist route. We waded through the throng, and finally reached the sanctum of the High Court. Roley was on another rummage into her past. Her relative, Piera Lal Roy, a barrister, had been one of the first attorney generals of Bengal. We wandered through the building unobstructed or challenged, searching for his name amongst the plaques that lined the interior halls of the court. One door opened and inside a smoke-filled room we glimpsed about twenty lawyers. A few looked up but no one said anything to us.

Jessica was enthralled by everything around her. When we talked about plans for the next few days, I mentioned a possible visit to the school I had attended as a child. 'We don't have to go,' I said. Her response was immediate. 'Of course, I want to go. That's why we came here, isn't it? I want to see your school. I want to see where you grew up. I want to see everything.' When we got to La Martiniere, it was closed but this didn't deter her; we found an open door that gave access into the building. She roamed the grounds, wandered through deserted hallways, and into the main assembly room. She scoured the names etched on boards with details of their accomplishments. 'Is your name here, Dad?' she asked. Captivated by the surroundings, she absorbed every detail from my past.

Wanno Haneveld was waiting for us in Delhi. Jessica and I had visited him in Holland, and I was so happy that, like Roley, he had joined us.

A few days later, on 13 January, we arose before dawn and set off for Agra, a city about 200 kilometres south of Delhi. Our hired car came with a guide who trickled information about the building of the Taj Mahal. The guide used his knowledge as a weapon of influence, and he wielded it to great effect, dishing out snippets of details in small doses. When we asked questions (Did the designer of the Taj Mahal really have his hands cut off to stop him recreating another architectural masterpiece?) he would sometimes ignore us or give a cryptic reply. The guide's smirks and silence annoyed us, particularly Jessica, who was devouring information about this beautiful and inspiring architectural masterpiece.

We were eager to reach Agra, but our guide insisted we stop near some market stalls for a 'break' and he left us in the car. Within minutes, a hawker appeared outside. He pulled a bear on a chain. The bear's coat was dry, the hair matted in places, and the animal appeared exhausted. The stick his master wielded looked sinister. The pusher rattled a begging bowl of coins and poked the bear with his stick, and it performed some tired and perfunctory routines. Someone called out not to hand any money over.

When it became evident that no rupees would be passed through the car window, the hawker started to beat the bear viciously with his stick. Each crack against the body of the bear was shuddering. 'Stop it! Stop it!' Jessica yelled, but couldn't stop her tears. We shouted out for the driver. He could tell we had rumbled his routine; the stop had probably been orchestrated with a kick-back for the guide from the distressing tourist 'attraction'.

The incident with the bear scarred the rest of the journey. But our spirits lifted when we arrived at Agra and parted with our guide. The Taj Mahal was a spectacular homage to love and grief. Yet, amidst the phenomenon of its architecture, it remains a bittersweet experience tainted by the recollection of a defenceless animal exploited by a cruel and ruthless owner.

A few days after returning from India, Jessica packed her car to return to university in Manchester. I walked with her to the front of our house where her red Peugeot was parked. She kissed my cheek. 'Thank you for taking me to India, Dad. I'll never forget the trip,' she said.

'I love you.'

We spoke a few words, and that special moment between father and daughter was lodged in a memory bank safe in my heart.

She got in the car and pulled out of the driveway. I stood in the street and watched the red car reach the end of the street and turn left.

She was gone.

# CHAPTER 5

# Living in the Moment

*2005 – 2007*

We were delighted that Jessica was pursuing her dreams of a career in fashion, and confident she'd be successful at university in Manchester. But our concerns were about the risks and challenges she'd face far from home.

For her first year, she lived on the third floor of the university's halls of residence. While the rules were loosely enforced by staff, it became evident that students became experts at evading them. Academic classes, tutorials, study leave and libraries weren't the only thing on offer. I knew she smoked, though never in front of me; we worried that she was getting intoxicated by the allure of a cigarette from a different kind of leaf. We became alarmed that the increase in her habit would have a detrimental impact on her health, but it was difficult to restrict her. I was anxious but didn't know what to do.

Jessica was enthusiastic about university life and worked hard at her course. In her second year, she rented a house in Manchester with friends from university. She phoned or texted me regularly, sometimes daily.

One of her assignments was to design and market a new product. I gave her an idea based around a party bag that she convinced her group to adopt. She called me after the presentation. I could hear the background chatter of students but everything else was drowned out by the excitement in her voice. 'We've just finished. I had to call you straightaway. They loved it. Thanks Dad.' Their tutor awarded the group top marks and a local marketing company approached them about taking it on as a commercial venture.

I was pleased with her success, but my reward was those few minutes on the phone.

In 2005, Jessica and her best friend at university, Rachel Hodgkinson, went to Zimbabwe. Jessica's boyfriend at the time Bruce and his family lived near Harare, and he assured us that the girls would be safe under his protection. We trusted Bruce and agreed. Jessica loved Africa and in Zimbabwe, she absorbed the local culture, travelled deep into the countryside, and adapted to a basic rural lifestyle. Later, her Zimbabwean friend told me, 'She made such an impression on everyone she met, even my grandfather still asks about her. No one who met Jess could forget her.'

In early September, after her car was stolen and before a replacement could be found, I drove Jessica back to Manchester in time for the start of the new term. On the M6 she told me about her experiences in Zimbabwe. On their last day, her camera had been stolen, taken by a maid in the house where they were staying. Jessica said, 'This girl was so poor. She had nothing. I pleaded for her. I asked them not to punish her. I just couldn't be angry with her. I'm upset that we have very few photographs from our visit.'

It took us about four hours to reach her student flat in Manchester. We unpacked her luggage and then drove to the supermarket to pick up supplies for the week ahead. She pointed out local landmarks, but the conversation returned to Zimbabwe.

'Those people have nothing, they're desperate. I want to do something, Dad.' Her voice was rich with fierce passion. 'We've got to tell people about what's happening. Do you think Hazel will help?'

I advised Jessica to work on a presentation for our friend Hazel Thompson, an award-winning photojournalist. But Jessica couldn't wait, so we phoned Hazel. When Hazel said she'd consider the idea, Jessica became excited. 'I want to go back to Zimbabwe with Hazel. I'll carry her bags. I'll do anything.'

I'd thought of taking the girls from her flat to dinner, assuming that it was a Dad-type thing to do. But I also coveted time with my daughter.

I followed her directions to Manchester's famous curry mile. She chose the restaurant. I remember where we sat. The curry she ordered was delicious; mine, not that much. She was talkative and animated. Her brown eyes sparkled. She told me she was excited about returning to university. I remember walking back to the car with her, driving back and parking outside the entrance which led to her flat. She leaned across and kissed me, 'I love you.' In the moonlight I watched her walk up the stairs to her flat and open the door. She paused for a moment. In that instant, the streetlamp lit up her silhouette, framed in the doorway. She waved and walked inside. The door closed.

* * *

Her determination and motivation were evident: on top of her university degree work, she enrolled at Central Manchester College and took night classes in beauty therapy, qualifying as a beautician. Throughout her second year, she worked part time as a mentor at an inner-city secondary school, helping troubled teenagers complete their studies. When home, during the holidays, she worked part time as a care assistant, helping the elderly and housebound in the local community. One year, instead of a holiday job, she bought a market stall and spent most of that summer selling clothes in places such as Blackbushe in Surrey, Europe's largest outdoor Sunday market.

She still found time to come to the office. One day the conversation became intense. 'We've got to talk seriously, Dad. Can I take over from you at Jubilee?'

She had the heart, passion, and ideas, but did she have the experience? I explained how organizations had a process to follow.

'I know.' She was adamant. 'But can we work that out? If you let me take over, then I'll stop everything else. This will become my main focus. This is what I want to do.'

* * *

During her holidays from university, we hatched plots for adventures and compiled a list of things to do, places to go. One summer's day we took the train into Waterloo Station, walked across the South Bank to our first stop, the Salvador Dali Exhibition at County Hall. Then across town to the Andy Warhol show at Tate Modern.

We wandered into the first exhibition on the ground floor. I strolled across the large space, surveyed the scene in a few minutes, and was ready to move on. 'I'll catch up with you,' she said. She was enthralled by the spectacle. After watching her, I too became absorbed. I was no longer in a rush.

The installation in the Turbine Hall was called The Weather Project. It was a stunning visual experiment. The ceiling was covered with a huge mirror, the air filled with a fine mist or fog. A gigantic orange globe hung suspended in space. It was like a setting sun. People were standing, others sitting, many were sprawled across the floor. It's difficult to do justice describing the scene. The effect was mesmerizing. It was intoxicating and dream-like.

Later I learned that we were among two million visitors captivated by the work of Olafur Eliason, a Danish-Icelandic artist. In the end, we had to force ourselves to leave, aware that time was limited.

When I heard Joan describe Jessica as someone who knew how to live in the moment, I recalled that trip, when I saw her live – and embrace the moment. But not just that, she drew me in to share the experience with her.

## 2006

I was sprawled lazily on our terracotta-coloured IKEA sofa. It hadn't been a particularly busy day. I flicked through the television channels and settled on *The Simpsons*. It was about 5.30pm. Another three hours to go. I rehearsed the familiar routine. It was the same whenever Jessica returned home from university. I'd head out to Victoria Coach Station on Buckingham Palace Road, park in my usual spot and wait for the Manchester coach to pull in. She'd text me along the way; the last message would say "c u 1min" or something like that.

But this was my last assignment. Jessica had finished university and was heading home. She was scheduled to be with us for three days, before flying to Malaysia with her boyfriend Ryan and his parents, for a family wedding. Jessica wanted to travel the world and she was excited about this trip.

I loved meeting Jessica. Driving home was always the same. 'What's the latest? Where's Rachel? How's Luke? What's mum doing?' She wanted to know everything – and fast. After the headlines, it was 'I'm starving.' We'd stop at the McDonalds drive-thru at Wandsworth or the pizza take-away in Battersea. They weren't the most popular, but they were the nearest.

My phone rang. I put *The Simpsons* on mute. It was Jessica.

'Dad!' Her voice said it all.

'What's happened, Jessica?'

'I've lost my suitcase . . .'

'Oh no.' My first thought was: clothes, make-up. I was about to say, 'We can replace that.'

'It had everything in it, Dad. Everything.'

And then came the bombshell.

'It had my final coursework for university. The entire term's work. My diary. My wallet. My bank card. All my money. All I have is my phone and the clothes I'm wearing.'

'Oh Jessica!' My heart started to pound. But there was more.

'It had my passport.'

My mind raced. But before I could connect the dots, she spelt out the consequences.

'I can't go to Malaysia.'

I'd swung through all the emotions in less than sixty seconds. But her despondency gripped me. I calmed her and over the next few minutes we worked out a strategy.

I telephoned the local police station and the bus company. I outlined the crisis: Jessica had stopped off to do some last-minute shopping. She wasn't sure if she'd left the suitcase in a shop or market stall or if someone had snatched it while she was distracted, or if it was still on a bus in Manchester.

Dad was now on the phone pleading for help for his daughter. Everyone I spoke to was understanding and sympathetic. Perhaps they had teenage children and recognized the panic in my voice. The kind policeman phoned nearby stations to see if anyone had turned in a suitcase. We tracked the bus she was on and traced the driver. Over the next hour, one thing became clear: the suitcase was gone.

I phoned Jessica on the coach and told her.

'Dad . . .'

'Jessica, don't worry, I have a plan.' I tried to sound confident. I was determined that she wouldn't miss the trip to Malaysia. I was going to do everything I could to fix the problem. The next hour was a flurry of activity. Phone calls. Enquiries. Addresses. Notes. Plans. And then the drive to Victoria to meet her coach.

Her text came in: Almost there.'

The coach pulled in. Jessica was one of the first passengers out. She rushed over to me. I hugged her. 'It's going to be all right, Jessica. We're going to work it out. Here's the plan.'

The first stop was passport photos. The next day we returned to London's passport office in Eccleston Square. We filled out the application form for a replacement passport. A letter written overnight outlined the urgency. And then we waited our turn. The tension was palpable as we queued at the desk. The clerk behind the counter glanced at us and reviewed our documentation. When he indicated that her application would be accepted, Jessica gave out an audible sigh.

Jessica contacted her tutor and explained the loss of her university work. He acknowledged that she was a good student, had earned her marks throughout the year. Significantly, he would accept a replacement document. Her final assignment had been an analysis of the French fashion brand Louis Vuitton. Luke was recruited to recreate the project, so she set about preparing copious instructions for her younger brother to follow. With financial enticements agreed, Luke took the job, though he probably would have done it for nothing. We were all caught up in the high stakes drama and everyone wanted to help.

Before she left, Jessica told me her Bible was in the suitcase. I said we could replace it. 'I know,' she replied. 'But that meant a lot to me.'

The past few days had been like a tornado. Suddenly, it was dawn and we were driving to Gatwick Airport to meet Ryan and his parents.

'I can't believe it,' she told me in the car. 'We did it! I'm really going. I didn't think this would happen. Thanks, Dad, for helping me!'

The trip to Malaysia fulfilled her desire to travel and Ryan's family loved her. She returned in March 2006 in time to prepare for graduation four months later, after completing her three-year degree in fashion buying and marketing.

Jessica was among several hundred excited students at the ceremony in Manchester. Joan and I were in the gallery of the auditorium. There was some mix-up over her identification in the rollcall, so her name appeared after everyone in her term. I heard her name called out and saw her stride forward to receive her graduation diploma. I felt so proud of Jessica at that moment. This was a landmark achievement in her life. We took her out for a celebratory meal and handed over our gift to mark the occasion: an iPod, the latest must-have product from Apple. She loved it.

But all was not well.

There had been a spiralling of difficulties within the Jubilee organization starting around the years 2005/2006.

This was unusual. We'd had fantastic people and mostly been free from internal disputes. When problems arose, they were resolved with goodwill. I'd considered the trustees of Jubilee Action were my friends and didn't pay close attention to the problems. Anyway, the office trouble wasn't my biggest concern.

I was disturbed but this wasn't about office strife. It was about Jessica. When she returned home after her graduation in July, she moved her things into the room Rachel had vacated.

At 19, Rachel had achieved one of her ambitions: to own her own property, and she had moved into a studio flat. She had a remarkable ability to focus on an objective and achieve it. This was a typical example of that resolve. Her flat was about fifteen minutes away, but I missed her, and shared this with Fr Shay in the Philippines. He emailed back: 'She has to fly away from the nest so that she can fly back.'

Her room in our house was on the first floor at the top of the stairs. It was decorated in her distinctive minimalist style with soft pastel colours of pink and mauve. I always thought of it as 'Rachel's room'. It took a while to get used to Jessica walking out of it. Yet, she stamped her brand on the room. Her declaration of intent was a poster on the door: Tupac Shaker.

Within days, it became obvious that she was troubled. She was erratic, unpredictable, detached, aggressive; her behaviour deteriorated over the next year. She seemed out of control and there was a noticeable decline in her ability to cope.

I didn't want to face it. I couldn't understand what was happening. Neither could I grasp her inner turmoil.

I knew that things weren't right. Perhaps the combination of wanting to experience and experiment with everything life offered without boundaries and the thrill of risk-taking was exacting its toll. Her disruptive behaviour and sudden rages were deeply worrying and caused tensions. We couldn't always agree on how to respond or what action to take. I'd never been so worried.

The fury seemed to come from nowhere. She worked part time as a care attendant. One Saturday afternoon, she mentioned the distress of an elderly patient.

'I feel so sorry for him. He doesn't have any family. No one visits him. All he has is a television and that's broken,' she said. 'I'm going to buy him a television or he'll have a miserable Christmas.'

We knew she didn't have much money, so Joan and I offered to contribute to the cost.

'I'm going to buy the TV now and take it to him,' she said.

'Why don't you check if he's managed to get one since you last saw him?' I suggested.

That was it. My question enraged her. She exploded in a shouting tirade that lasted over an hour. If I stepped out of the room, she followed me. It ended with her storming out and slamming the door.

The arguments increased in frequency and force over the year. Once started, she couldn't stop. In one disturbing incident, a glass was smashed. In another, the police were called.

That year showed how serious things had become. The next, 2007, wasn't any better. This passage of time stretched us and took us to the limit. It almost broke us amidst distressing scenes at home.

We attempted counselling. She reluctantly agreed to enter the Priory Centre in Surrey for cannabis addiction and we dropped her at the clinic one afternoon. I was relieved at the thought that she would finally get professional treatment. The experience left me so exhausted that I fell asleep when we returned home. Not long after, I was awoken by Joan. There had been an incident. We had to go back for her.

She was diagnosed with schizophrenia and prescribed strong medication. She was sectioned briefly at the Abraham Cowley Unit at St Peter's Hospital in Chertsey. I visited her daily but usually I sat in the car outside the building, praying. I had to summon all my emotional strength to enter the facility. I was relieved when she was discharged, though desperately anxious about the future.

'I'm going to go travelling,' she announced suddenly, but wouldn't give any details.

I prepared myself for her sudden departure. I imagined getting a call one day from someone somewhere about my daughter. I told myself to be ready to leave at short notice to reach her and bring her home. I contemplated stopping work to look after her. She was my daughter, my beloved daughter. She was hurting, in distress. But this was beyond my experience. I didn't know what to do or how to help.

A few days later, she declared that she was going to get a cat. I was against the idea until Joan suggested that caring for a pet could help. 'It might put her off travelling,' Joan said.

Jessica visited the RSPCA Millbrook Animal Centre in Chobham and saw several kittens in an enclosure. A black kitten with paws that looked as though it was wearing white socks rolled over in front of her, clearly playing to the gallery. She named him Indiana Gandhi Zion (Indy).

One morning she asked me to drop her at Woking. We drove there in silence. I parked near the station and put a £20 note in her hand. She gave me one of her special smiles. I stayed in the car and watched her walk towards the town centre. She looked lost and vulnerable. It was a haunting image.

Despite the turbulence of her mental health issues, she faced every challenge life threw at her with faith, courage and determination. As her father, I struggle to record this period of her life. Even now, this is painful. Even those affected by the symptoms of her sudden illness speak only of warm memories of past times with her, and confirm the strong imprint of Jessica on their lives. I am determined that this period won't define her but will be a footnote to her story.

Amidst the turmoil, there were tender moments. She was clearing out her room one afternoon when she came to me with a book. 'I know you'd want to have this,' she said. It was *Home for a Bunny*. It was a memory from her childhood, her favourite bedtime story that I'd read to her numerous times.

When a day passed without incident, I desperately hoped it marked a turning point.

She worked every temporary job she could get. The night before starting a new post, I'd drive her to the location so that she knew the route. Her love of animals and birds remained. She bought a bird bath and feeders and placed them around the garden. She agreed to work with me on an overseas volunteer programme for Jubilee Campaign. When Fr Shay visited us, we all went out for a meal and she talked about going to the Philippines.

In late December 2007, my phone rang. It was Jessica. 'Dad! Reverend Devaraj just phoned me.' The excitement in her voice was unmistakable. 'Guess what? I was telling my friends about our visit to India. And then he called.'

We talked about her visit to India and Prem, the young boy near death who had touched her heart. Prem was recovering slowly. 'He's a miracle child,' she told me. 'I want to go back.' Her voice was rich with emotion as she spoke.

Zimbabwe was on her mind. She continued to try to persuade me to do something. She phoned Hazel Thompson and (unknown to us) arranged to visit her over Christmas. A meeting was fixed for 29 December.

We closed the office for the Christmas holidays, and I drove home on the last working day, relieved to gain some respite from the disputes within the charity (Jubilee Action). But my mind returned to Jessica. When I reached the Old Woking Road about ten minutes away from home, I couldn't stop the tears flowing.

Christmas morning passed without incident. After lunch, we settled down to watch *The Christmas Story* on DVD.

I found myself distracted from the film. The position of my seat was directly in line with Rachel and Jessica, who sat together on the opposite sofa. All I could do was look at Jessica, and that profile of her is before me as I write this. I felt an overwhelming compulsion to concentrate on her and to pray for her. 'Lord, help her.' I repeated the words silently to myself.

It is the strongest and last memory I have of Jessica.

# CHAPTER 6

# The Worst Day of My Life

*27 December 2007 – 10 January 2008*

I awoke on the morning of Thursday 27 December 2007 with a darkness in myself, a sense of foreboding, something I can't explain.

I thought I was keeping my feelings hidden, buried deep within. Our friends, Janet and Craig Rickards, dropped in unexpectedly late morning to borrow Joan's mobile battery charger. Later they told us that I seemed upset and wondered if they had annoyed me.

We hadn't heard from Jessica all morning so after they left, we decided to rouse her.

Her room was locked from the inside. We called her name. There was no answer. My knuckles hurt as I banged on the door. There was no answer. Her poster of Tupac Shaker looked down on us.

Joan came up with several suggestions. My throat was dry, my mind faltering. I couldn't think. Joan got a screwdriver and started to unscrew the bolts that held the door of her room together. Finally, we just pushed it open.

I felt something holding me back. I couldn't look and walked the few paces to the bathroom around the corner and waited there.

Joan entered the room. She yelled out.

My legs wouldn't hold me. I crashed down. Some strong driving force passed through my body. I thought my heart stopped for a second. 'No Jesus, no!' I cried out loud.

I couldn't enter the room.

Joan spoke to me from inside the room in a strong but calm voice, 'Dial 999. Call for an ambulance. Say there's an unconscious female casualty not breathing in the house. Tell them I'm doing CPR on her.'

I followed her instructions.

'Open the front door wide,' Joan called out again, in that voice of restrained authority, as her nursing training kicked in. 'Make sure there's nothing obstructing the entrance. Keep a look out for the ambulance. When the paramedics arrive, tell them it's the room at the top of the stairs.'

The phone rang. It was Craig.

'Hi Danny, there's a problem with the charger. Do you know . . .'

I interrupted him, 'Jessica's passed away.'

I put the phone down. I had been weeping since I heard Joan first call out but only fully realized this when I found it difficult to speak to Craig. A deep ache entered my body, a pain in my chest.

I stood outside the door to Jessica's room. I could hear Joan's physical movements as her hands moved on Jessica's body. 'Breathe, Jessica, breathe,' I heard her say.

The ambulance hadn't arrived. Joan told me to call 999 again. I did. Within minutes, two ambulances pulled up outside at great speed, brakes squealing. They parked across the pavements on either side of the street. Two medics raced up to the house. I stood aside and followed Joan's instructions exactly.

'Unresponsive female. The room at the top of the stairs.'

The men sped forward, taking the stairs two at a time.

I remained downstairs in the living room. It was difficult to stand. My mind was emptying itself of thoughts and words. I heard the medics footsteps on the stairs coming down. They were walking, not running. One of them entered the living room where I stood. He put both his hands on my shoulders: 'I'm sorry.' His voice was thick with emotion. There were tears in his eyes.

I became aware of Craig and Janet in the room. They told me later that they assumed that the medic knew me from the way he spoke.

The medic told me, 'I know what you're going through.' I was looking at him, but his words were being scattered across the room, lost in the air, blowing away. His hands gripped my shoulders. 'I lost my daughter also. Not exactly in this way, but it was similar.'

He spoke to me for a few minutes.

The medics called the police and waited in the house till they arrived. They're not allowed to leave an unexpected death. The police gave us permission to enter the room and left. Janet and Craig said they had to finish some things and would return.

There were only three of us in the house. Joan. Me. And Jessica.

Joan told me that it would get busy. 'We should say goodbye to Jessica while we are alone in the house with her.'

She went into the room.

I had lost all feeling within myself. It was as if I'd lost my balance and could fall at any moment, but it was happening in slow motion.

Joan came out of her room. It was my turn. I trembled, yet somehow found strength to step into her room.

Jessica was lying on her side on the bed. She was peering through the glass window that almost covered one entire wall. She was looking out at the sky, the clear blue sky, the great beyond. She looked calm, peaceful. It was as though she was dreaming.

I cradled her in my arms. I remembered the first time I held her this way. I recalled how it felt, how my world changed, how joyous I was. I had been waiting for the moment when I could hold her that same way again. Now I was weeping. My tears fell on her face. I wiped them away with my hand. Gently, tenderly.

I spoke aloud to Jessica with words and tears. But the words 'Goodbye Jessica' wouldn't form in my mouth or in my consciousness.

\* \* \*

Joan was upset but could think. 'Phone Rachel.' 'Get Luke.'

Luke at 18 had taken a job at Woolworths in West Byfleet. Craig drove to pick him up. Luke decided to walk. They missed each other.

Rachel had just arrived in Leeds to visit Joanne Lawrence. She had been our next-door neighbour for several years and the girls had stayed in touch after her family moved north. Joan called Rachel but didn't tell her exactly what had happened. She was worried about Rachel driving over two hundred miles, after getting such shocking news. So I phoned Joanne's father, Graham, and asked him to go into a room on his own, somewhere where no one could hear him. I told him what had happened.

'What did you say?' I heard him call out.

I told him again.

He shouted out loud.

After we ended the phone call, Graham and the family gathered around Rachel to comfort her. She didn't have any cash money, so everyone in the house threw their wallets and purses on the table. Pound notes and coins were counted out, enough to get Rachel a ticket on the first train to London. The train was scheduled to arrive at King's Cross station at midnight. Craig offered to drive to London and meet her.

I felt in such turmoil. Every few minutes I had to stop, take a breath. I couldn't believe what had happened.

I wanted to tell my mother personally, so Craig drove us for the 15-minute journey to Horsell. Janet stayed behind at our home. No one spoke in the car.

My mother was startled when we arrived unexpectedly. I took her hand, and said, 'This is the worst news I will ever bring you.'

I told her.

She stared incomprehensibly at me for a moment. 'What are you saying to me?'

The shock forced her out of her chair. 'I can't believe it. I won't believe it.' She spoke as though saying the words would make the truth a lie. I repeated it. I struggled to get her to acknowledge something that I couldn't accept.

Janet phoned: the police were waiting for us. The ambulance from the mortuary had arrived. They had come for Jessica.

We left my mother and Clement deeply upset. Outside the evening light had gone and we drove back in silence through the darkness of the night. As we turned the bend and approached our house, I saw a vehicle parked outside. It was a large silver Mercedes. I stared at it for a moment. This was the vehicle that would take my beloved daughter on her final journey from our family home.

I raced inside. I wanted to carry her out myself. Someone told me that the service people had to do it. I didn't have the strength to resist. I watched them bring her down on a stretcher covered with a white sheet. I walked with them to the Mercedes.

I became aware of two men in suits standing in front of the house. While I was standing outside and Jessica was being carried into the vehicle, someone called out to me. 'The police are waiting.' I ignored the information and stood by the Mercedes. The two men who had carried my daughter out of our home shook my hand and walked to the front of the vehicle.

I placed my hand on the Mercedes. Somehow, I thought I could mysteriously reach inside and touch Jessica. I wanted to speak, but I was in shock. My tears fell on the street. The Mercedes started up and slowly pulled out. I watched it reach the end of the road and turn left. I had stood in this exact place many times in the past when Jessica left home for Manchester. And then, hours later, the text would come. 'Dad. I've arrived. Love you.' This time there would be no message. My phone silent.

I walked slowly back to the house. The policemen saw my distress and said they would return the following day.

This would be the last time Jessica left our home. It was the worst day of my life.

* * *

I didn't sleep that night. None of us did.

The next day wasn't any easier. I couldn't think of anything else except Jessica. I felt her presence wrapped around me.

My mind was in turmoil. I still had that sensation as though something – something physical – had left my body. It was as though a raging storm had ripped through me, like a rushing wind stronger than the strongest tornado that devastates a house leaving nothing inside, only an empty shell of a structure that in time collapses. If a thought entered my mind, it lasted a few seconds and then this flash of Jessica jolted me. I thought I would fall to the ground at any moment. I had to hold on to a chair to stop myself from crashing down.

I just couldn't believe what had happened. I walked from room to room. I saw things that belonged to Jessica all around me. I thought my fingers would be scorched if I touched anything of hers. I couldn't look at anyone. I felt my body shake. My eyes burned.

I came to think of this unspeakable and unbearable event as an earthquake in my heart and life.

I had been in an earthquake in Mumbai. I was in an airport hotel on about the tenth floor when I was awoken. The whole room shook, the pictures on the wall rattled, the glass on my bedside table fell to the ground. I was half asleep but stumbled across the room, holding onto the furniture for balance. I don't know how long the tremors lasted. The building seemed to shake for several minutes but it was probably only a few seconds. I opened the door and stood in the doorframe. A few other guests were in the hallway. No one panicked, and it passed.

When I felt dizzy and thought I was losing my balance, that incident returned to my mind.

I was buried under the rubble of memories. Images from the past hurtled towards me like pieces of concrete and fell on me. I would turn and feel her standing beside me.

Joan said, 'We've got to tell people, her friends.' She was right, but the thought filled me with dread. My mind took me to 27 February 1985 when Jessica was born. I couldn't wait to tell everyone. Now, this day, 27 December 2007, over twenty-two years later, it was the last thing I wanted to do.

Joan was brave and made a start. I couldn't stay in the same room to hear words that tormented me. I stood behind the door, listening to the sound of her voice. As I heard Joan speak, it came to me that I was Jessica's father. This was my child, my beloved daughter. I didn't want anyone else to take my place in her life. I had to affirm my role as a father. In doing so, I would embrace her as my child and claim her for my own.

But I didn't know how to move forward. How could I speak to people and tell them this terrible news? Yet there was a growing conviction that this was what I had to do. I was reminded that I had taken joy and strength in my identity as a father. The idea started to overwhelm me. This was my destiny. This was the role I had been born to fulfil as her father.

The pain and ache didn't lift, neither did the tears. But I felt something cover me. I was in a thick fog and I couldn't see far down the road. It was a small step, a hard step, but the only one I could take – to tell her friends.

She had three phones. I made a list of her friends and wrote their numbers alongside their names.

I dialled the first number. I recognized the voice of the girl on the phone. After I told her, she screamed. I heard the phone being thrown on the floor. Another friend said, 'No! That can't be true.' Someone else yelled at me, shouting down the phone, 'What are you telling me?'

I was in our kitchen and dialled another number. 'Is that Lucky?' I asked. Lucky had been her boyfriend just before she started university. Jessica told me he was 'a sweet boy'. After he moved to Scotland, we never saw him again. 'Yes, I'm Lucky,' he replied. 'This is Jessica's Dad,' I said. Then, I told Lucky. He was deeply upset, and I found myself consoling him. I said, 'I'm so sorry to give you this news.'

There were times when I didn't believe what I was saying. My mind drifted off. This can't be true. This is not happening. But it was happening. At times, I was somehow detached, floating above and watching myself go through this strange series of phone conversations. Other times I became clear-minded and lucid. I knew what to say and communicated clearly. In the next instance, everything fell apart. I moved between these two with ease. Sometimes this happened mid-sentence. Everything going well. And then bang.

She's gone.

And then I was jostled back to reality, forced to deal with the practical things of everyday living.

Sometime that afternoon the policemen returned. We sat at our dining table while they asked questions about my daughter. We did our best to respond. It was their job; they were professional but sensitive. She was so young. This was so sudden. As a result, there would be an autopsy and an enquiry. It was routine, they said. Routine? Not for us.

Janet and Craig stopped in. The following day was Craig's birthday, but he brushed it aside. They took charge. Their four children were temporarily on hold; Erin was just eight years old. If we needed something, it was done. When I was anxious, I would see them, and a sense of calm settled on me.

Flowers and messages started to arrive, filling the house. I studied every card and letter as if it was a question at an exam. It was humbling. People had taken such care in their words. Friends I hadn't seen in decades. Others were just casual acquaintances. Some didn't know us but heard about the tragedy. Even though there was nothing anyone could do, the messages meant a lot.

One afternoon, some friends came to visit. I saw their car pull up and went outside. My friend called out my name jokingly from the street. I shrank back into the house.

Roley phoned from Jerusalem and asked if we'd fixed at date for the memorial service. It was to be on Thursday 10 January 2008.

Craig and Janet arranged for the service to be held at their church, St Paul's in Addlestone. The vicars, Reverends Ben and Chris Beecroft, opened their doors to our family, and church members welcomed us like old friends. Our focus over the next week was to prepare for the service. Jessica had faith, but she hadn't been a regular churchgoer. We didn't want a formal religious meeting but something that was true to her and reflected who she was as a person.

Janet suggested that we meet daily as the day of the service drew nearer. She compiled a list of things to do; when we thought of something, it was Janet (and Craig) with friends from St Paul's who made it happen.

It was decided to have a display of photographs and souvenirs that covered the stages of her life. So, one evening, we gathered in our living room to choose photographs to be used. Someone would call out, 'I remember when . . .'. I found the experience too difficult and frequently left the room.

Roley arrived from Jerusalem three days before the service. She said, 'This is part of the Jewish tradition. We stay with the family in mourning.' Frequently, she'd be in the kitchen preparing food for friends who'd dropped in. One evening, I was standing in the doorway weeping. She touched my arm; 'Hurting?' All I could do was nod my head.

A few days before 10 January, we had the idea of showing a collection of video clips during the service: Jessica roller-skating when she was about seven; the sisters dancing on holiday; in London to see the beached whale. But no one could think of how to get the footage copied in time.

'I'll do it,' Rachel said.

Rachel drove to a computer shop in Woking, but they didn't have the relevant equipment. A customer in the shop overheard the conversation and stepped up. He took Rachel to his office and completed the transfer of video tapes for her.

Sometime that autumn, Rachel had introduced us to Matt, her new boyfriend; even a passing encounter showed how much in love they seemed. Matt had a sensitivity about him, as he shared the sadness that had fallen on her, and united with a family in mourning

Rachel set up a tribute page for Jessica on Facebook and this reached school friends from Fullbrook, and others. The local newspaper interviewed us; as a result, Jessica was featured on the front page of their next edition.

No one felt like eating, but one day Rachel expressed an interest in strawberries and blueberries; a few hours later, Joan's friends from university arrived unexpectedly with a large bowl of blueberries and strawberries. Through such acts of kindness, we had the sense that we were being supported by the prayers of people. That God was holding us.

\* \* \*

The night before the service, we met at St Paul's to make the final arrangements. The orders of service were set out on the seats, the visual displays arranged. At the keyboards, Joel Rickards played a selection of songs including 'Blessed be Your name'. Rachel said that it was one of the songs that she and Jessica sang at the Coign Fellowship in Woking which they had occasionally attended. Later, a friend whom we hadn't seen in over a decade visited us. She brought us hugs and a book by Matt and Beth Redman: *Blessed be Your name.*

Our intention for the service was to celebrate the life of Jessica. We were heartened to hear of prayers and special services that were held around the world to remember her: in Olongapo City, Philippines; Mumbai, India; Kenya, Turkana, Africa; Manaus, Recife, Rio de Janeiro, Brazil; Andijk, Netherlands; Belfast, Northern Ireland; and in Merida, Mexico, the oldest cathedral in the western hemisphere, dating from 1547.

And in Addlestone Surrey, over two hundred people joined us at St Paul's Church at 1pm on Thursday, 10 January 2008 to demonstrate that Jessica was deeply loved.

Friends travelled from Jerusalem, Washington, Belfast and throughout the UK. The church was silent, as everyone stood while we walked in and took our seats. Jessica was before us at the front of the church. Dozens of red roses on the casket spelt: 'JESS'.

Reverend Beecroft set the tone with a gracious welcome. We sang 'Blessed be Your name' and 'This little light of mine', a childhood favourite. Roley recalled moments from Jessica's childhood. Her Zimbabwean friends and Rachel Hodgkinson from university shared recollections, Hazel Thompson wrote a poem for her entitled 'A Light Went Out Today'. The poem started,

'You left this world so suddenly, I didn't get the chance to say goodbye.' Lynieve Austin, from M People, sang 'Amazing Grace'. Valeri Barinov read Scripture. With that soft lilting Russian voice, he reminded us that there is an appointed time for everything. A time for every event under heaven. A time to give birth, and a time to . . .

Mark Rowland, Jubilee's former Assistant Director, titled his address 'A Tribute for Jess'. Mark said:

> She intuitively took the side of the under-dog. I know how proud she was of being part of Jubilee's narrative of fighting injustice.
>
> She was also courageous. I remember being on a train with her and getting into some detailed discussion on ethics or religion. It upset the man sitting across from us and he interrupted – telling me I should keep my opinions to myself and not impose them on Jess. Before I could respond and much to my relief, Jess looked at him with a hint of disdain and told him, 'I can think for myself, you know.' That was Jess – like an arrow straight and true – never afraid to engage in the big issues and never afraid to speak her mind.
>
> But I also saw that courage when Jess was ill. I got a phone call from Jess a few months ago after I hadn't heard from her for a long time. She was calling from hospital, but she wasn't afraid to reach out and let me know she needed a friend.

It meant a lot to me that George Verwer made time to join us. George had been a mentor, but also my friend through difficult times. Here he was again, on a day that had the power to crush me, by my side. He told the congregation that there were people all over the world who were praying for us and for this service. George's searing prayer stirred the church.

Craig Rickards played a special composition on his Yamaha 61 soprano saxophone that he had written, accompanied by Joel on keyboards. He titled the melody: 'For Jess'.

I wanted to be the last to speak, the last to say her name out loud.

I had been weeping through the service. I didn't know if I would be able to speak. It had been suggested that someone else could read my speech; of course, that was impossible. My heart was strong, my mind resolute. I had to stand in front and take the lead when we celebrated her life and said our earthly farewell to Jessica.

I walked to the pulpit and looked across the hall. As my eyes settled on specific people, I wondered if I would be overpowered by emotion or silenced by tears. But in the first few seconds of standing in the pulpit, I felt a calm descend. I reached out to embrace this final public moment between father and daughter.

I thanked Ben, the vicar and friends at St Pauls. Then I told the congregation

Jessica chose this church. When Rachel and Jess decided to attend church together, they went to the Coign Fellowship, but Jessica had first suggested this church to Rachel when they'd driven past the building some months before.

And now, here we are.

I spoke first to Joan.

> You gave me three cherished gifts and created that sense of family that changed me, brought a kind of healing to my life. We have two gifts with us, Rachel and Luke. Today we give back one gift to God . . . Jessica.

I told people that no drugs were found in her body and there was no evidence of self-harm.

I acknowledged my struggles.

> I am angry. Why has this happened? Why Jess? Why Now? I want to find someone to blame. I feel I carry some of the blame.
>
> But every moment I spend in this dark place is a moment that I am not celebrating the extraordinary character Jessica was. We declared at the start of the service: A time for every purpose . . . She would be the first to say, Don't look back, Dad. Let's do something together. So after, this day, you will never hear me speak like this again.
>
> There are tears. There must be tears. But there is no despair.

I tried to convey what she was like as a person, and what she achieved in life.

> Jessica was a born leader with natural confidence. If a problem arose, you knew she'd find a way to fix it.
>
> Jessica was born running, and went full force, eager to try every new experience. And she could

barely finish one before wanting to start another. It wasn't that she'd start lots of things and leave one incomplete while taking up something new. She had a strong work ethic and you could rely on her to get the job done.

She had an inner confidence that propelled her forward. No matter what scrapes she got into or what trouble and havoc was caused, nothing deterred her from her pursuit of her objective. Once Jessica had set her mind on something, nothing – and no one – could turn her away.

Jessie was a big character. She knew who she was. She gave herself 100% to whatever she was doing. She embraced it, became engrossed in it. Joan put it well: she knew how to live in the moment, a defining comment about her character and attitude to life. She accomplished a lot, always ready to try new things. When I cautioned her one day about some new challenge, Jess turned to me with a blaze in her eye, 'Dad, do you know anything I've started that I didn't complete or couldn't do?'

Jessica didn't just pass through this world. She wasn't a passenger on this journey across the landscape of life. She wanted to stop the train when she chose to, when something caught her eye, to explore it and pick it up. Then get back and go forth into the future.

Jessica never missed a chance to tell me that she loved me. There were texts or emails that appeared unexpectedly, or after we'd been together.

I carried one of the cards that Jessica sent me and held it high, though I didn't read out her message. It felt too personal, something private between father and daughter.

I urged people in the congregation to take every opportunity to tell friends and family how much they are loved. It's not enough to assume people know how you feel about them.

While preparing my eulogy, I reflected on the great outpourings of love extended to us. But this was not everyone's experience. I expressed it this way:

> Jessica was loved. And the people with us in this church are a demonstration of that love. But what a sadness for those who have passed away with no one to grieve, with no one to hold them close or to love them in the way that Jessica was loved. Who pass away, and no one notices. Some from an error and no fault of their own, others from violence, in the wrong place at the wrong time. Who fall in a foreign land, far from home, who pass away for a cause they don't believe in or know little about or falsely believe will bring glory. Who pass away with no knowledge of God. What a sadness that brings.

\* \* \*

Somehow, I made it through to the end without faltering. But I had struggled while preparing my eulogy. How could I describe Jessica in a way that fully conveyed all that was in my heart, what she meant to me, and the impenetrable and indescribable loss that I felt? How would she describe herself?

Jessica had used my computer regularly. I would return home and find her at my desk. Nothing was said. It was just understood between us, everything that was mine was hers. She had written and stored her CV on my computer, and she updated it regularly. Here's an extract that communicates some of that drive and initiative. She was 19 at the time:

> In the summer of 2004, I set up and ran my own business, a market stall selling young women's fashion. I purchased a small van, a market-stall frame and a range of garments from suppliers in the 'northern quarter' of Manchester. I went to market roughly 4-5 times a week, around the area of London, including Kempton Park, Farnborough, Blackbushe, Reading and Woking market. I employed people to work for me and was totally dependent on myself for the success of my business. I found the experience extremely challenging and hard work but at the same time very enjoyable and rewarding. It has definitely given me great experience and insight into the field in which I hope to go into (fashion retail). I have learned a lot about fashion as well as business.

I remember how excited she was when she bought that market stall. She set it up in our back garden, and recruited Luke and a friend to join her team. You just couldn't say no to Jessica.

'First-Born': that's how Jessica signed her messages to me sometimes. She would speak that out. That special look in her eye that passed between us, that glint that said, we're special, you and me.

My days out with Jessica when she was a child were the happiest of times. Cherished memories. It was usually at the weekends or on a holiday. We'd get in the car and drive for miles, windows down, music turned up, the breeze blowing her long hair every which way ...

Now, I find myself sometimes staring into the distance. I think on those days a lot. How I felt at the time, my heart overflowing with happiness, filled with a sense of contentment. I experienced life as it was meant to be.

I was reminded of a memory from her childhood when we lived in Cobham. Jessica was six. Her black hair down to her waist. She'd been unusually quiet and then turned to me, her big brown eyes looked directly at me and said:

It's not fair. I want things to stay just the way they are at this moment. With Durango (our cat) still with us. With Nannie and Grandad. You, Daddy, just the way you are now, Mummy looking just the way she does. Rachel and Luke, the same size. And me, still six. I want our family to be just the way we are at the moment. And never change.

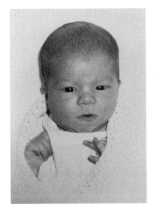 

First Born –
27th February 1985.

With Peter Benenson
(Amnesty International founder).

Writing 'I Love you' to Mummy.

A wonderful surprise at Heathrow after three weeks in South Africa.
I still have her 'Welcome Home Daddy' banner.

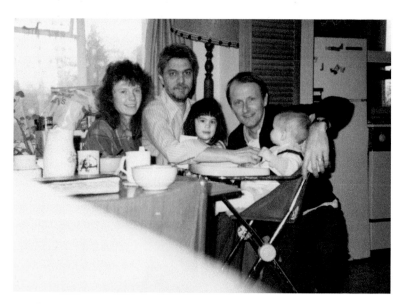

My friend and mentor George Verwer.

Christmas visitors: Tanya and Valeri Barinov.

Our family in Cobham.

The Jessica Corporation's official membership card.

In time.

Artwork for our campaign.

Her t-shirt says it all.

Cuddles for Monty.

Horsing around with Luke and Rachel.

Jessica, aged 10, with her young friend Soren Rickards.

From Jessica's album titled 'Rescued Birds'.

Hugs for Treacle.

Making the front page.

Proud grandparents.

I love this photo of Jessica.

Cadet Jessica Smith at her passing out parade.

Making her mark.

Campaign event in Holland with Alice Diamond, Jubilee Campaign NL director.

'Jessica – what a lovely name!' Billy Connolly.

School prom. She looked like a movie star at a film premiere.

Catwalk model and a producer of this London College of Fashion show.

A garland at the Jubilee Homes in India. Reverend Devaraj never forget her.

Jessica (front row) at the Jubilee Homes.

With the desperately ill young boy at the shelter in India.

Jessica's photograph of a cobra in Mumbai.

Family together.

Jessica on her 18th birthday. I love this image.

In Zimbabwe. She was determined to help.

I was so proud of Jessica when she graduated
from university.

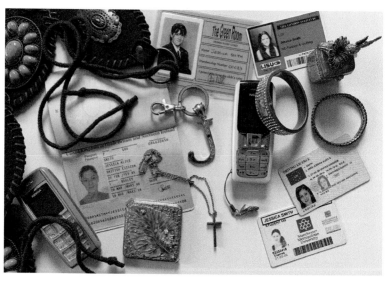

Memories of Jessica.

PART TWO

# JOURNEY

# CHAPTER 7

# An Earthquake in My Heart

*10 January 2008 – 27 June 2008*

The service at St Paul's Church fulfilled our mission to celebrate Jessica's life.

Janet Rickards had the idea that the ceremony should include an act of remembrance, something personal yet practical, that involved everyone. It was decided to give each person a red helium balloon as they left the church on their way to Addlestone Cemetery on Green Lane, about a mile away.

Ben Beecroft led the short and simple ceremony at the cemetery. It was referred to as 'the committal'. The word made me shudder every time I heard it mentioned or saw it written down. It didn't get any easier at the graveside. At the end, I heard myself call out, 'Miss you Jessica. Love you Jessica.'

At some point, we released our helium balloons. I looked up and saw the balloons, coloured dots of varying sizes, bouncing and dancing as they rose, like red tear drops across the blue sky.

Afterwards, we returned to St Paul's church hall and met our family and friends. Tears were the only response I had for everyone who greeted me with kind words and tender hugs. The hall was crowded but I felt alone. A line from my favourite book (*The Little Prince* by *Antoine de Saint-Exupéry*) came to my mind: 'It's such a lonely place, the land of tears.'

I couldn't find much to say and found myself repeating the words, 'I can't believe this has happened.' I was in a constant state of shock. Someone told me that my speech 'was the most powerful expression of pain and love that I have ever heard.' Jessica's school friend Elizabeth Richardson said, 'It must have been the toughest speech of your life.' Yes, Elizabeth, it was.

The memorial service for Jessica was held on the second Thursday in January. The evening had turned into a cold, dark, unfriendly night. The stars were out as we stood in the courtyard of the church car park and said our goodbyes to family and friends. Most likely, some were deciding which route to take for the journey home, negotiating the M25, with work the next morning, plans for the weekend, the usual things on any normal day. Except for us: normal had lost its meaning.

Kitty Thompson returned to Belfast that same evening. Friends drove Roley to Stansted Airport for her midnight flight back to Jerusalem. Ann Buwalda returned to Washington the following day.

Rachel asked Matt to drive her to Hayling Island. She'd wanted to go somewhere that reminded her of Jessica and this was one of the last places she recalled where the sisters had been happy together. Matt was a tender companion and they stayed there as darkness fell.

Rachel felt close to Jessica. From the depth of the night sky something stirred her soul with a strong connection to her sister, as though Jessica was reaching for her, wanting to make things right. The evening sea breeze brought with it a chill, but also a reconciliation with the past. For Rachel, it was a time when childhood wounds were healed, a moment of cleansing.

The hours after the service were crushing. When everyone had gone, the hall was cleared, the floor swept, chairs and tables put away. Joan and I were the last to leave. We drove away in silence.

When we reached home, I turned the key in the door and stepped inside. The house was cold, dark and empty. It mirrored how I was feeling.

There were several messages, texts and emails. I skimmed through the names, reading words but not taking much in. I opened an email from Kate Thomas. She had worked as Jubilee's fundraiser in the 1990s. Years later, when I was walking on North Street in Guildford, I heard my name being called by a mother with three children. It was Kate. I'd seen her a few hours earlier at Green Lane Cemetery when she introduced me to her husband. I shook his hand but didn't look at him. I wept as I read Kate's email:

My husband described it as 'the most powerful and moving service I've ever been to.' Although he never knew Jess in this life, he says that he felt he got to know her in the service. I think there was a real sense of her presence there. We both cried at many points. When we got home I heard him describe the service and talk about Jess to his work colleagues on the phone; he said, 'Jessica achieved more in 22 years of life than most do in 80, she had brought more good to the world than I ever have in my life, it was truly humbling and made me want to change my life.'

Kate's words pierced through the desolation I was experiencing.

I moved around the house, restless and unsettled. Wherever I turned, there was a memory of Jessica in every room. Familiar places turned into memory stations, places we'd laughed or argued or hatched plots or plotted adventures. I vividly remembered the evening when she burst into the living room looking for me, 'Dad! Let's do something tomorrow – yeah?' There were cards and messages and letters and flowers in every available space in the house. I picked up a card and read the message but couldn't focus on the words and stared at it incomprehensibly. Nothing was getting through. Nothing made any sense. Nothing would or could bring ease in the moment.

Later, I reread the messages. I learned how her life had reached many. In some instances, the touch may have been light, but the impact had endured. I picked out the ones from Jessica's school friends. I'd known them as children and watched them grow into young adults. When I saw them at the service, it took me back to the days of Jessica's childhood and teenage years. I loved the messages that recalled experiences they'd shared together.

Elizabeth Richardson wrote:

I still can't believe this has happened. It always meant a lot to me that she made the time and effort to see me every time I came back to Surrey for a visit, and to visit me at my house in Lincoln. I won't forget all the time we spent at school together, I was really glad to have known her. I remember her speaking about your charity quite often so she must have been very proud of the work you do

Richard L'Estrange:

What an absolutely brilliant tribute service to Jess. The most personal and memorable service I have ever been to. I think about the adventures we went on. We had so many plans to do so many things. Now we'll never get to do them. I loved the way she liked to do things on the spur of the moment. A couple of times she took me to one of her favourite places with a ruined castle in a field. The last time we went, there was a sudden storm and we both got totally saturated. When we went to Ladies Day at Ascot, Jess was thrilled when someone in a kiosk painted her nails for free. I found a photo of us on a beach when we went to West Wittering. Our dinghy got caught in a current and we had to hang on to a rescue boat to get towed in. I never met anyone like her. She was one of a kind. Such an inspirational person in my life. I miss her so much. My life is empty without her. I will never forget her and miss her forever.

I questioned how people of faith responded to personal tragedy. I knew Chacko Thomas from OM, but hadn't seen him in decades. He wrote:

> Nearly five years ago I had to let my son go to Jesus, he was 17 years old. People still ask me why? I have no answer. I do miss him but have left it for God to answer as and when he pleases. But heaven has never been so important to me. I do sometimes fear that I want to see my son more than wanting to see Jesus, I am sure He understands.

I wondered if Chacko's faith had overpowered his personal feelings. Then I read on:

> No one can take the place of our loved ones, not even God. He has His own place in our lives. But He gives grace to cope, although grace is not anaesthesia, the pain remains.

Chacko's words rang true. I didn't know much of grace; I was discovering something of pain.

Fr Shay Cullen shared a personal experience:

> I am only trying to understand your loss and hurt, by recalling when someone close to me passed away – my mother and my eldest sister. I cried. I still feel that hurt or loss from time to time . . . I try and relate to the passing of Jessica and what it is like for you . . . but your loss is even greater, and I can't come close to it . . . so I can't understand it fully . . . Jessica was so young, and very special and her spirit is and always will be with us.

Fr Shay recalled a visit when Jessica talked to him about travelling to the Philippines, 'I am happy with the memory that we had a little time together last trip . . . that's precious. And we shared a meal together.'

Kate Thomas wrote again. She spoke about the loss of her father:

> I remember when my dad died very suddenly – I was 12 – the days seemed to blur into nothing – it was like I was dizzy from it all, and simple things like eating to television and radio – to big things like church and the meaning of life – all of them made no sense any more – worse, they seemed only emphasize my pain rather than take it away. It was as if I was suddenly completely lost, yet the world continued to spin round me – I wondered if I would ever find my way again . . . or even if I wanted to. I did, eventually, and you will too – but it is a slow journey, one you will make in one way or another for the rest of your life. I often think that the real pain of the cross was not what Jesus went through – but what the Father went through, watching His son die.

I was so pleased when Ryan, Jessica's boyfriend, texted me. Ryan was tall, lanky with soulful eyes. I was fond of him.

> Today was a beautiful service. Jess would be so proud. With Jess I have the best memories of my life, she was so beautiful. There is such a storm in my heart and when I feel her, I can't move. The speech you made was so moving. When I was watching the video, I saw her drinking some tea, it

so reminded me of her. I loved all those little things. I could watch her do the most casual things and just fall in love all over again. I miss her so much. I aim to be just like you in my life, to know and understand what really matters. Thank you for all the kindness and love you showed me. I will carry a part of Jess in my heart always.

A few hours later, Ryan's second message came in:

I miss her every day, so much. I haven't been in touch with God in my life but now I ask God to look after Jess every night. I'm sure He does. I thank God for giving me those years with Jess, best years of my life.

Jessica had been so excited when Ryan's parents invited her to join them for a family wedding in Malaysia. How we laughed about that dramatic incident on the drive to Gatwick Airport. And that moment in the terminal when Jessica said goodbye . . . It was packed into my memory bank. Ryan's text brought it all back.

Later, Ryan's cousin from Malaysia wrote:

When we heard the news, we were just heartbroken and remembered the time, however short, that she shared with us. We had great fun with Jessica and she truly became a part of our family. We really feel honoured to know her.

Ryan's aunt sent this message:

When Jessica came to Malaysia in March 2006, it was to attend my son's wedding. I am indeed very sorry for your loss. I just cannot accept it until today. Since Ryan called me, I have been looking at Jessica's photos taken with us. I never for once thought that it would be a memory and that we will never meet her again. During the short time she was with us she became part of us – enjoying all the Malaysian food and culture. She was so fascinated with the wedding, we Sikhs have so many traditions and she was amazed. I can remember all the hugs I gave her as she was leaving never to know that I will not see her again. Thank you for allowing Jessica to come to Malaysia and sharing your lovely daughter with us. She will always be in our hearts. I can only say that God loved her more.

Jessica's trip to Zimbabwe left a lasting impression. Mrs Bernadette Charewa, her Zimbabwean friend who was living in the UK, told me how attached she was to Ronald, her youngest child.

I did not know I was pregnant with Ron until 27 weeks. Because I have a heart condition, I was having scan after scan at St Peters Hospital in Chertsey. Jess made sure she took me to hospital so many times, sometimes staying with me for long hours. No wonder there is such a strong bond between the two even in death.

Bernadette's daughter Glenda confirmed this:

She fell in love with our Ronald before he was even born. Because of him, Jess is a household name in our home. When she spent a weekend with us the two had a wonderful time. They would play in the bath until water starts flowing out. Unfortunately, Ronald is too young to understand death and still thinks his friend Jess will come and take him to the seaside as she promised.

Bernadette told me, 'Glenda can never celebrate Ron's birthday without shedding a tear for Jess. When Ron's homework was to write a letter to someone special, he wrote a letter from the heart to Jess.' Bernadette recalled that Jessica had taught Glenda to drive, and that their family in Zimbabwe 'remember her for laughter and theirs when she was eating some of our Zimbabwean dishes.'

Bernadette made this observation, 'Jess was a kind of friend who was always there for you when you need her. My point is Jess lived her life as if she knew she had a short time. It's no consolation but she left a legacy.'

Jessica had taken an active part in our campaign for James Mawdsley, a prisoner of conscience in Burma and his courage stayed with her. James sent us this message:

I cannot imagine how painful this is for you. Oh Danny, this must be the hardest cross to bear. May God wipe away every tear.

Sam Burke (inspired by James and David Alton) volunteered in our office. He wrote:

When I used to work at Jubilee on Fridays, Jess was always the first to welcome me, and the first to offer me a lift to the station – even though it was out of her way. She was always great fun: willing to share a joke and ridicule the office politics! I remember her once telling me on the way home, how proud she was of you and how she admired Jubilee's work. After a long interlude, I was delighted to see Jess at the book launch (for James Mawdsley). In our brief chat, we exchanged news and she seemed to be on great form. I'm sorry that meeting shall be our last, in this world, anyway.

Sheila Walsh, the singer, author and TV host, emailed me from America:

> I have no words to describe the pain I feel in my heart and soul for you. I cannot begin to imagine the grief that must overwhelm you.'

Brian Woods from True Vision met Jessica in passing. He wrote:

> Words feel inadequate at a time like this. We will be thinking of you and hoping that when the time is right you can move through the pain and on to remembering and celebrating the 22 years you shared.

I felt humbled by the effort people had taken in their messages. It put me to shame as I reflected on the dishonourable part of myself and what little thought I'd given when writing or sending cards to people in times of trouble. I'd scribbled a few words, scrawled my name and that was it. I'd scarcely given such communication a second thought.

\* \* \*

Janet gave me a list of people who had helped with the service and I wrote a note to each one, and to everyone else who'd sent us messages, cards, flowers and gifts. The message was the same:

The shock of losing Jessica never leaves me . . .

And that was the overwhelming sensation: Shock. It was there in the morning when I awoke and lasted till sleep overtook me. It seemed that my mind had emptied itself and I could think of nothing except the events of 27 December 2007. It had become the centre of gravity and the reference point for all my thoughts.

I wanted to be involved with everything related to my daughter, yet I found it difficult to leave the house by myself. I needed Joan at my side. Everyday things that mean little suddenly took on great significance. The mundane task of closing her bank account made the facts just as real as a tombstone or memorial leaflet.

We drove to Woking and parked in the town centre. I clung to Joan's hand as we walked to the local branch where Jessica's account was held. I could hardly speak but I wanted to bear witness to this profession of loss. To the bank, she was another customer, account number 7436521, but to us, our precious daughter. With the procedures completed, the bank official confirmed: account now closed. The number with her name would probably be buried in the bank's archive. At her home, hearts breaking, terrible thoughts released in the dead of night. How will I ever get over this? Can I get over it?

I just couldn't imagine the days ahead or what life would be like without her.

Then filling in forms to cancel her magazine subscriptions to *Vogue*, *Elle* and similar publications. Jessica signed up for every offer and every invitation. Her name and contact details were submitted for deletion but once you're on file, you turn from an individual into a statistic, sold and resold. The phone rings. Someone in a call centre speaks her name. They want a few minutes of her time. She'll want their latest offer. Despite registering with the telephone preference service, the calls persisted. I recognized the signs: the tunnel-like sound effect, the background chatter, the hollow voice, then the salesperson calls out the name that appears on the screen in front of them: Jessica Smith. But to hear her name spoken by a stranger was chilling. The phone calls went unanswered. I watched the phone ring and ring. The sound sent a shudder through me. This inanimate object, this telephone, had turned into a tormentor.

I stood by our bedroom window and looked at her car, the silver Escort, parked on the street opposite our house. I imagined how the scene played out on 26 December. After visiting friends, Jessica got into the car, strapped on her seat belt, placed the key in the ignition, turned on the engine and eased the car into first gear. Then she drove home.

* * *

The autopsy on Jessica's body didn't reveal the cause of death. They found no evidence of drugs or of self-harm. But since her passing was so sudden and unexpected, and because she was so young, an inquest was to be held, scheduled for March 2008, put back to July.

Michael Burgess, of the Surrey Coroner's office, was in charge of her inquest. Mr Burgess was the deputy royal coroner. He'd been responsible for the inquest on Dodi Al Fayed in 1997 but withdrew from that role in July 2006. We gave permission for tissue samples to be taken which were sent for investigation; more information would be provided at the inquest. Another official from the Coroner's Office talked me through the process. He spoke about Jessica with such sensitivity. It was as if he had known her, but also understood how I was feeling. He told me, 'We'll look after her as long as she's with us.' His words meant so much to me.

Professor Rajiv Hanspal, a consultant physician, one of my closest friends from my youth, tried to help me understand more: perhaps the recently changed dose of Jessica's medication could have had side effects that caused this tragedy. His counsel was intended to console me. But even if the inquest informed us of the exact reason – the facts, the only fact that I knew was this: she will never again walk beside me in this life.

The Coroner asked us to prepare a Life Statement, something that summarized her life. He put it this way: if in the future, someone asked the question 'Who is Jessica Smith?' they would turn to this document for their answer. The Life Statement went to the heart of the matter and touched on all my fears. To write this would be to acknowledge the very thing that I struggled to accept. Still, I knew that this was a challenge I must rise to. This would be the statement that defined Jessica.

And there was no one else that I could allow to take my place and prepare a document that was to represent her life. I was her father.

If I thought time would stand still, I was wrong. Friends didn't forget us. In India, Reverend Devaraj had arranged a Christmas party for the children in his care but after I'd phoned him with the news, he cancelled the event. In Liverpool, David Alton and his family remembered us at church on the Sunday after our memorial service. He wrote:

> Dame Julian of Norwich famously said that 'all shall be well and all things shall be well.' I wanted to say that to you when I called on Sunday but didn't feel it was the moment. But I do believe it and as my children lit their candles for you on Sunday morning, I felt that Jess is now well and perfectly at peace. It was the feast of the Holy Family and the homily was about the many vicissitudes that they faced as a family – and how we are not immune from the same sort of suffering.

Valeri Barinov emailed me, 'Today is already one month as the Lord took Jess to His side. I want to encourage you and all of your family with the words of Jesus.' Valeri passed on a verse of Scripture, and then wrote, 'We have all come to this world as guests for a while and then return to God ...'

\* \* \*

On Sunday 3 February, 24 days after the memorial service for Jessica, Joan returned to St Paul's Church for their 11am meeting.

155

After she left the house, I stood in the living room amidst the cards and flowers. Jessica's cat Indy was curled up on the window frame. The stillness in the empty house was punctuated by the occasional rattle from the radiator of an old and creaky central heating system.

My mind went to Rachel: her determination after the memorial service to go to Hayling Island, a place that reminded her of Jessica. The thought of doing something similar came to me and the longing intensified within a few minutes. But I couldn't settle on any destination.

Gripped by the idea, I pulled on my thick black winter coat, grabbed the keys to the Passat and headed outside. I felt a compulsion pushing me out of the house, like a scene from a Hollywood movie when the action hero charges from a burning building where a bomb was about to explode.

I was in the car, still without a plan. As I turned the key to start the engine, I felt an impulse to drive to Green Lane Cemetery.

I was relieved that the car park at the cemetery was empty. It meant that I would be alone with Jessica. On previous visits with Joan, people passed with that same gist of sadness in their eyes, a coded message that we each recognized.

Her grave was covered with flowers. The emotions of the past few days were overwhelming, though I felt comforted in this private moment of solitude.

I noticed some movement behind me and saw a young couple. I couldn't tell where they were headed but I didn't want to face anyone, including these strangers. I decided to leave and kept my face hidden, unable to glance in their direction.

I heard someone call my name. 'Danny.' It was a girl's voice. I heard her say, 'You're Jessica's Dad, aren't you?'

'Yes, I'm Jessica's Dad.' I was surprised at how strong my voice was. It felt good to speak those words: Jessica's Dad. 'Thank you for coming,' was all I could muster, and I hurried away, back to the safety of my car.

But before reaching the gates of the cemetery, I pulled the car to the side. Who were these people? How did they arrive at this particular moment? I had to find out more. A few minutes later, their car appeared, and I heard their story.

Daniel told me Jessica had asked him to DJ a party while she was at university in Manchester. Sophie explained that Daniel hadn't been able to get time off work to attend the funeral service, so she'd driven him to the cemetery this morning. Then Sophie said, 'I never really knew Jess. I only met her three or four times. But I can't get her out of my mind.'

I thanked them for coming, 'Hold happy memories of Jessica.'

They drove ahead of me and left the cemetery. A car turned into the grounds, so I waited until the vehicle passed. These extra minutes gave me time to reflect on the timing of our meeting. I hadn't intended to leave the house, in fact, I hadn't been out on my own since 27 December 2007. Yet, on the spur of the moment, about thirty minutes earlier, I'd set off for Green Lane Cemetery, my first ever visit alone. At the same time, Daniel and Sophie had driven to the cemetery. A few minutes' delay on either side and we would have been strangers in cars passing at the gates of the cemetery, not knowing we shared a common bond.

I felt exhilarated by the unexpected encounter. I started to laugh, the tears rolling down my cheek. It gave me a kind of release. That restlessness I'd felt when leaving the house had diminished. I now felt settled with a calming presence of God, yet still bound with overwhelming, unspeakable grief.

While I was at Jessica's grave, an image from her childhood came to me. The wall at Ripley.

I drove to Ripley, parked, and found the bridge. I stood by it for a while and looked across at the fields. Almost nothing had changed, though the wall was smaller and lower than I had remembered it. Jessica held my hand. Her long black hair down below her waist swayed gently as she moved, step by step across the bridge. How she trembled as she clung to my hand and stepped forward. And how I trembled, worried that she might fall and injure herself.

I placed my hands on the bridge. The stones were cold to the touch. I felt the wintery chill move through my body. That memory from almost twenty years ago became alive in my heart.

* * *

January and February were difficult months and there were consequences in the days that followed. Joan resigned her place at university, leaving her course in counselling; Rachel worked two jobs, but she struggled and couldn't sustain both. It was tough on Luke; he stopped work and became reflective and withdrawn.

I didn't know how things would unfold between Jubilee Campaign and Jubilee Action. In February, a correspondence started with Jubilee Action's trustees. The office issues seemed to be happening to someone else.

Rachel's 21st birthday on 10 March was the first time we'd been together as a family without Jessica. Janet Rickards visited with three of her four children: Soren, Anna and Erin. Rachel didn't look well. Matt was attentive and protective. Everyone did their best to help Rachel through this special occasion. I was part of the group but felt distant. The absence of Jessica was like a pounding in my head. I imagined her sitting on the sofa with us, hearing her distinctive intoxicating laugh.

The following month, an artist friend offered us one of his oil paintings as an expression of affection. His sweet gesture went unanswered.

On 24 May, Mathilda Armstrong, a friend from OM, sent us one of her hand-made cards, an exquisite creation that had the ability to lift the spirits. She wrote: 'It's been almost five months, but it must seem like yesterday. We can't measure such loss by time.'

Mother's Day and Father's Day passed. Neither Joan nor I had the energy or inclination to celebrate an occasion that had once held importance for us.

Joan's birthday was June 26, but this also slipped quietly away, remembered but unmarked. The following day, June 27, was exactly six months to the day, yet to me it seemed that only six days had passed.

I drove to Green Lane Cemetery with the scenes from 27 December 2007 being enacted in my mind. The Moment. The ambulance worker. Visiting mum. The silhouette of the policemen standing on our doorstep. The steel grey Mercedes van from the undertakers parked in the street outside our home . . .

There was a time when I couldn't imagine going to the cemetery. Now I'd become a regular visitor. I wanted to be near Jessica, to be in this place where her earthly body remained and from where she would never leave.

Jessica was at the far end of the grounds, in the last plot, number 25, an area roughly twenty feet by about sixty feet. The main road inside the cemetery was a single track for cars and at the end the pathway on the right led to Area 25. It seemed at times separated from the rest of the cemetery, tucked away from the city and from life. It felt hidden from the world, a kind of protected garden where a row of trees at the far end formed a green partition. The sound of humanity moving about: the golf course on the other side were reminders that life carried on. And if the seclusion became too overwhelming, there was the driving hum of the M25 motorway.

On an earlier visit, I'd noticed a man tending a grave in Area 25. When he first approached, he saw that I was too upset to speak, but later, we talked, and it comforted me.

'This is such a beautiful spot,' he said.

We spoke in the shade of a nearby tree. He named the trees, and as we talked, a bird flew low over us and settled on a nearby branch. Jessica would have loved this spot, with the birds swooping and darting past. He said, 'There's every kind of bird here: sparrows, robins, pigeons, crows, woodpeckers . . .' He told me about the people buried in the cemetery; some had owned land near the grounds; the well-known traveller and his wife, with a large plot on the left-hand side near the entrance. 'Rod Hull is buried here,' he said, as he walked me down the path and pointed out the grave of the television personality known for appearances with Emu, his puppet.

Another day, a man tending a grave nearby stopped. He was tall and rugged but spoke in a soft voice, 'It's peaceful here.' He pointed to the grave of his father and said that he owned the plot around the grave. I felt brave enough to speak and told him we'd bought the place alongside 'my daughter'. I wanted him to know that Jessica was here, and that I was her father. We spoke for a few minutes, and then he walked on. 'Enjoy the weekend, as much as you're able to,' he said knowingly. And I understood the hidden meaning of his words. Once you stepped onto this patch of earth, you can't walk on and just re-enter the world as though nothing has happened.

On this summer's day in June, the cemetery seemed tranquil. I had this sense of being surrounded by love. I set off amidst the rows of tombstones, glanced at the graves amidst the overgrown tufts of grass and weeds and ferns. I saw the names, dates, words, flowers, souvenirs. Everyone buried here had people who loved them. Some lived nearby, others in far-flung lands. When their names were mentioned, their friends and family smiled, they were remembered with love and affection. To me, it felt as though some of that love remained behind in the atmosphere, and I was breathing it in.

I walked along the side path amongst the overrun plants and untended graves. I stopped at one of the tombstones and read the inscription:

In memory of Leslie Viney
Died aged 21
1909 – 1931
From a loving wife
And son he never knew

Mr Viney's wife and son weren't named but the engraved text filled me with sadness.

I recognized a man that I'd seen walking down Green Lane while driving to the cemetery. He spent some time at a nearby grave, then headed towards the exit.

I wondered about him. Whom did he visit? Did he live nearby, or had he travelled far? Maybe he'd come from Addlestone railway station, or from the bus stop on the main road? Whatever the answer, he had walked a great distance, because there was a part of himself that he'd left behind in this place.

I think that was what happened every time we visited this burial ground. We left behind a little fragment of ourselves. And people who think of Jessica, and remember her with love, send a part of that love. It touches all who walk these footpaths to get to her resting place in Green Lane Cemetery.

And perhaps that's why the cemetery holds that aura of serenity. It carries the sense that deep love abides there. It flows through the little pathways and passages. It embraces all who sojourn on its grounds; some for just a few moments, others for eternity.

# CHAPTER 8

# Everything Changed

*2008 – 2009*

The world still turned but everything had changed. I didn't think the situation between Jubilee Campaign and the charity we'd set up some years later (Jubilee Action) could get any worse. But I was wrong. I was also wrong in assuming that the issues would be resolved if we all got around the table and talked things through.

Fr Shay Cullen tried. He flew in for a pastoral time with us and visited Jessica's grave. The next day he met with Jubilee Action trustees. Fr Shay had personally investigated the issues and prepared articles for publication, available to anyone who contacted him. Reverend Devaraj visited the UK with a similar objective. So did Ann Buwalda from Jubilee Campaign USA. There were telephone calls, letters, emails, meetings, and further discussions with others, with even more complicated twists and turns.

Andrew Smith, a northern businessman, had been instrumental in establishing Jubilee Action as a charity and served as its first chairman. Things between us had been strained at times but when I explained the situation to him, it was as though nothing had happened. He recommended that we seek legal advice. It seemed extreme, but later we realized it was wise counsel.

After false starts with disorganized and inefficient law firms, I turned to an old friend, the barrister Paul Diamond. I hadn't seen Paul in years but followed his career in high-profile cases such as his defence of the Egyptian Coptic Christian penalised by British Airways for wearing a cross. Joan and I met with Paul on 9 July 2008 in chambers near the Bank of England. Although it was upsetting to realise how far things had deteriorated, we felt reassured with Paul offering strategic direction. Meanwhile, Kirsty Lewis, from Thomas Mansfield Solicitors, handled the day-to-day process. Paul and Kirsty were outstanding. Efficient, sharp, and just what we needed.

The day after the meeting with Paul, we headed to Woking for a 10am appointment. It was the day of the inquest.

When we arrived at HM Coroner's Court, four reporters were waiting in the lobby of the courthouse. Joan and I were called into the offices behind the courtroom to meet the coroner who questioned us about Jessica's medication. When the formal inquest started, Joan spoke first, and then it was my turn. The hearing was methodical and precise and lasted about forty minutes. The assessment acknowledged the dosage of medication was influential and played a part. The verdict: Accidental death.

The reporters crowded around us outside the court. They were sympathetic but suspicious. One said they had never been to an inquest where anyone had met with the coroner before the official hearing had begun. I stood in the street and answered their questions until everyone was satisfied.

A few days later the newspapers hit the street. The local press featured my photograph of Jessica in her scarlet red prom dress on the front page. The *Metro* printed the same image.

I drove to Woking Railway Station and took bundles of the *Metro* from the metal rack outside and read the story in the car. I stared at Jessica's image. I closed my eyes and pulled the paper onto my body. I walked back to the station for more copies of the *Metro*. I didn't know what I would do with the extra copies. This was the paper that Jessica read on her journey into London, and occasionally carried home. Now she was featured in the paper. Its three million-plus readers saw my photograph and read the story of Jessica Smith . . .

I looked at Jessica's photo in the *Metro* throughout the day. Every time I turned to that page, the shock hit me as if it was the first time. Yesterday's meeting with Paul Diamond came to my mind. I thought of phoning Paul and cancelling everything.

\* \* \*

The problems between Jubilee Campaign and Jubilee Action's trustees dragged on for another eleven months. Incredibly, the whole experience took a total of eighteen months, and finally came to a halt in June 2009. Paul was responsible for the final negotiations: an out of court settlement that culminated in a confidentiality agreement signed by all parties. This meant both sides were banned from discussing the details.

For us, the implications were stark. We didn't have our database of about 25,000 people. I had developed this mailing list, which I started compiling in 1983 with Siberian Seven supporters. We'd also lost access to the charity's income of about a million pounds. My name had been on every fundraising appeal and donors had a personal connection to me. Suddenly, I was no longer able to communicate with them because all contact had been cut off. Without this huge resource, we wondered if we could continue. Would Jubilee Campaign have to close down? What would happen to the Jubilee Homes? How could we help Fr Shay? Was this the end of our dreams for Zimbabwe?

One day, when discussing our future, Joan took my hand and said, 'We had nothing when we started this work. It was just the two of us. We'll go back to that. We've got each other. That's the most important thing.'

It was simply the most wonderful affirmation of love, something that I will never forget. Over the past few months, I had grown to depend on Joan more than ever before. Her encouragement meant everything to me in that low moment.

And that's what happened. We went home and started up again. We registered Jubilee Campaign as a charity. Joan established the organization's administrative hub in Luke's former bedroom. Next, we attempted to build a database from, well, almost nothing. We didn't have a master plan but were heartened by people who drew alongside to help. They know who they are, and we will always be grateful to them.

At some point over this period, Joan had a prophetic word:

Faced with starting over from scratch with no funds, resources and denied access to our database of supporters, was daunting. Should we even try to continue after everything that had happened? As I prayed, I felt the peace of God descend on me, and with it the realization that, I had been focussing on things that are insignificant to God. Funds and resources? A database? He created the world! God is omnipotent and knows the names and addresses of all who belong to him, and those who don't. If he wants something done, then a database of ten is enough – it just needs to be the right ten.

I felt God urging me to read Gideon's story. I turned to the book of Judges uncertain if this was God or just me recalling an appropriate story for our situation. I hadn't looked at the passage in a long time and was shocked by what I read.

Gideon was in hiding from an enemy that was destroying the people of God and everything they worked for. That is how he came to be underground threshing wheat in a winepress and not out in the open air of a threshing floor.

It was into this hiding place that the angel of the Lord appeared. The angel's words to the frightened man were: 'Hail mighty warrior, the Lord is with you.' Nothing could have been further from how Gideon was feeling at that moment. His honest response was, 'If the Lord is with us why have all these bad things happened to us . . .'

There is not a single verse in the Bible that could have more adequately expressed how I felt at that point in time.

God's response to Gideon was simple. He didn't offer an explanation or promise or even comfort. Just this: 'Go in the strength you have . . . am I not sending you?'

The next thing God did was to reduce the size of Gideon's army till there was practically no army left. Why? Because it was not Gideon's fight, it was the Lord's. No one could say Israel was victorious because it had the mightiest army – it won because it had the mightiest God.

We had been reduced to almost nothing. But the message was clear: God was still sending us out in His name to fight. The Old Testament fight was against a literal army. Our resistance was against poverty, injustice, oppression, evil . . . everything that Jesus came to restore.

Joan's prophetic word emboldened our spirits. But it was challenging.

The immediate pressure was money. We reduced our personal income to the bare minimum: however, this didn't cover our expenses. Again, the indefatigable Joan (Saint Joan, I called her sometimes) addressed the issue. She took a job working nights with the nursing team at St Peter's Hospital in Chertsey. This team of nurses provided social care in the community to ease the burden on Accident & Emergency units. They visited elderly patients and those needing attention at night. This wasn't high profile, but it was critically important for the community and the effectiveness of the National Health Service (NHS). Some years later, when the NHS budget was cut, the administrative posts were maintained, yet such vital but less visible services were reduced.

I don't know how Joan found the strength for this added night work. She was already busy during the day in the campaign office and home duties, including DIY chores, something I was less than totally useless at.

I closed the chapter of my life that involved Jubilee Action and didn't look back. It's not in my nature to wring my hands over what might have been or to agonize over regrets. This was in the past and I never returned to it.

I wrote to people who had been praying for us over the past eighteen months. I explained that my role with Jubilee Action was over. I was now rebuilding Jubilee Campaign. It was a twister of an explanation since the confidentiality agreement stopped me from revealing any details, and I intended to honour that contract. Still, the criteria of success would be if I remained true to the mission that God had called me to, rather than the size of our income or database.

I met Fr Shay in 1992 and our first charitable project was developed with him. He released us from raising funds for his work, and wrote, 'Stay strong, and stay in touch.'

Reverend Devaraj depended on us and I was upset that I couldn't continue our support. Jubilee Action offered him funds and I urged him to take them. But he turned them down. 'Our relationship is with you,' he told me on the phone from Mumbai. 'We trust in the Lord. He will provide.' His words humbled me. They also troubled me. Jubilee Campaign was in severe financial trouble and faced an uncertain future. Further, I felt exhausted, my mind distracted, my body weak.

Our priority was to restructure and stabilize the organization. We returned to our original principles and used 100% of all donations as designated, without deducting anything for administration. Devaraj arranged for us to be the conduit for UK donations, and we passed on the full amount that anyone sent for him. Meanwhile, Joan continued to work with the night nursing team at St Peter's Hospital to make sure we could pay our bills every month.

Sometime during the eighteen months while negotiations with Jubilee Action were continuing, David Alton invited me to lunch in the House of Lords. It was the first time since 27 December 2007 that I had been in London on my own. I was looking forward to seeing David, but it was a difficult trip. Just being in Waterloo Station was tough. In WH Smith, I spotted *Vogue* and *Elle*, magazines that I'd often taken home for Jessica after being in London. The feelings were so intense that I had to walk out of the shop.

As usual when visiting Parliament, I walked from Waterloo Station across Westminster Bridge towards the House of Commons. When I passed familiar landmarks, my mind filled with images of a day that Jessica and I had spent in London, our last time together in the city that she loved.

David was kind and did all he could to lift my spirits. But I was filled with an ever-increasing sense of despondency. At Waterloo Station, I learned that my train was delayed. In the past, I'd browsed at one of the nearby bookshops. This time, I couldn't face it. Neither could I return to WH Smith. I stood amidst the rush of life as people surged across the railway platform. One man flicked through the *Evening Standard*. A young woman checked the departure board. The 3:35pm to Orpington: delayed. An elderly man wheeled a brown tattered suitcase across the concourse. A young couple strolled arm in arm, oblivious to everyone around them. Life rolled on.

Two years had passed. I recalled the words of a close friend who told me, 'Time is a healer.' He lost his wife a few years earlier, and I knew that he meant well. 'Maybe for some, but not for me.' My abrupt reply had surprised him.

The passing of time hadn't brought comfort. The previous two years hadn't been focused on our grief. Instead, we'd become entangled by the issues between Jubilee Campaign and Jubilee Action. Yet that meant little to me. I was consumed by the absence of the person most precious to me – but there was nothing I could do about it. She wasn't here, and that wouldn't change.

I didn't want to pretend that things were alright or that they would get better. I recalled my interview with the Polish writer Jerzy Kosinski. I asked Kosinski how he approached the creative process. Did he just start at the beginning and push through till the final page? He replied, 'My discipline is to detect the mood of the moment.' I interpreted his words this way: 'Trust yourself. Your instincts.' I related this to how I was feeling.

Fiona Castle, the widow of the popular entertainer Roy Castle, shared her personal experiences with me. 'Two years?' she said, after hearing how long it had been since Jessica passed. 'That's nothing. It won't be easy. Expect to be tired. Exhausted. Be kind to yourself.'

Her words resonated. There wasn't going to be any quick fix. Neither did I want patronizing slogans and sympathetic words, even though they were well-intentioned and came from good people.

I struggled to leave the house. I clung to Joan. When the Rickards had a birthday party, I forced myself to join everyone out of a sense of duty or obligation. It wasn't a lot to expect to travel a half mile for a special occasion. But the evening didn't go well. I cringed every time someone spoke to me. I couldn't explain why I was too upset to speak. And when I spoke, I was dismissive, bordering on rude.

The contradictions raged within. I had things to say yet I was silent. I couldn't find words. I couldn't find my voice. I felt broken and crushed inside. I became distant and detached, and frequently this huge surge of loss hit me. It was involuntary and happened unexpectedly. I heard this described as the aftershock of grief. My world and everything I knew had changed. Suddenly. Instantly. In a lightning flash. Faster than a speeding bullet.

I read that in the game of chess, every move we make changes the way the world exists. And that's how it was for me. Planet Earth kept turning with people chugging along, going about their affairs. But the world that I knew didn't exist in the same way as it had done previously. I couldn't go back to how things used to be, and I didn't know if I could find a way to live amidst the way the world existed now.

I always knew that I'd face bereavement. But I didn't know what it would be like until I reached that hour on 27 December 2007. When lightning fell. Now, my daily experience was absorbed by her absence in our midst; the knowledge, the fact, that fact – that Jessica will never again walk by my side. This truth increased in intensity as each day passed. The road got longer, the weight got heavier, the night got darker.

I wanted to shout her name. I couldn't speak her name. I didn't want to hear the name spoken by anyone else. I turned off the television if a character was called by that name. For me, there's only one person with that name. I couldn't sit in my usual chair or watch the same television programmes or listen to the music I had played, or pick up a book by authors I once read. Jessica was an integral part of my world. She was always present inside my mind. She's in my thoughts as I wake and my final thoughts as I drift into sleep.

The mission of Jubilee Campaign and the pursuit of justice had given purpose to my life. I was frequently humbled by what had been accomplished, working with people such as David Alton in Parliament. I thought I was making a difference and 'doing something'. Yet through the years, my life had been enriched beyond measure. I was blessed above anything I could have imagined. I'd never got up in the morning and thought, 'Work today.' But now it was different and difficult. The calling hadn't shifted or decreased, but work felt like a duty.

For the first time, I didn't know what to do. I felt detached and adrift from everything that connected me to life. I had lost my ambition, the motivation that propelled me. I lost confidence and didn't think I could do anything for myself. I had this growing numbness, a feeling that I was too far down the road and I would never find my way back. Nothing mattered any more: who I was, where I was going, what I was doing or wanted to do. I couldn't think about anything else beyond my loss. I didn't want to see anyone or do anything. I felt dismayed that I had let down people such as Reverend Devaraj and Fr Shay and others who were counting on me. I tried to work but could only manage small tasks. I didn't want to think about what it would be like tomorrow or next week or next month, because I already knew the answer to my self-imposed question.

Some probed, others sought answers or a progress report, meaning well. With those I am close with, no words were needed, and the silence was enough.

The best way to dodge the bullet and to avoid people getting close was to always have a disguise and a mask ready to hide the deeper part of myself. It would keep all but the most inquisitive from my door. So it was that when someone asked, 'How are you?' my reply was, 'The same.'

I had reached the point where the passing of Jessica, and the process of grieving, would absorb me for some time to come, and probably never leave me.

\* \* \*

Music had topped my Christmas list in 2007. But after that December day, the music stopped, and my gifts lay untouched; the songs only heard when Luke was in the car and he'd snaffled CDs for the journey.

The first time I was drawn out of this emotional deep freeze was listening to 'Adagio for Strings' by Samuel Barber. I sat enthralled with my eyes closed. The rich powerful sweep of this music spoke to my spirit and reached me in a way that no words could. Mahler's Fifth affected me the same way. For several days, it was the only musical sound I heard.

In December 2007, I'd been listening to Elvis in the car. Later, I removed the CDs and returned them to the shelf where his music was filed in chronological order. Although Elvis had been my childhood musical hero, it was in the late nineties that I had returned to his music. I think listening to songs from my youth was a way of retracing my childhood.

Sometime after December 2007, I stumbled across a *Rolling Stone* magazine featuring the photographer Annie Leibowitz. I had seen her backstage at a concert in Central Park in New York where I'd interviewed one of the performers. Leibowitz had set herself the challenge of photographing an image that represented Elvis and I was intrigued by this premise: since Elvis died in 1977 (aged 42) what could she capture thirty years later?

Leibowitz's photograph became the front cover of her book *American Music*. It showed an old-style record player with an acetate recording on its turntable that had been in Elvis's bedroom on the day he died. The record was by the Stamps, a gospel group who toured with him from February 1971 until his final performance on 26 June 1977. I loved that photograph because it solved a mystery I didn't know was there: what music did Elvis turn to on the last day of his life?

When I saw Leibowitz's photograph again, it reminded me of an Elvis record from my childhood, a song that hadn't compelled me at the time. I didn't need to play the tune to bring it to my memory, but it sent me in pursuit of the origins of the music.

The song was written by Thomas Dorsey. He'd played barrelhouse piano in a speak-easy controlled by Al Capone in Chicago, accompanied blues legend Bessie Smith, and had a hit called 'Tight Like That' (with Tampa Red). When his wife died in childbirth, and their child followed two days later, Dorsey was overcome with sorrow. In his desolation, he turned to the piano for solace.

'Precious Lord, take my hand . . .'

The melody was based on an old gospel hymn from 1848 but the words came from deep within.

The tragedy was a turning point in Dorsey's life. He turned his back on pop and in doing so, his musical instincts re-energized musical traditions in the church. While Ira Sankey coined the term 'gospel music' in 1875, it was the dynamism of Dorsey's rhythms that popularized a new form of gospel songs. Not every church welcomed the mixing of religious lyrics with jazz music, but Dorsey's innovative musical arrangements made him a towering figure in the movement and set him in the forefront of the genre that linked gospel with the blues.

I'd read about how therapists used music in the healing process but never imagined that one day I would take my place within that circle. I tried to imagine how Dorsey must have felt. He'd used the sorrows of his own experience to create a song that outlived him and through the ages inspired many. Now it reached out to me.

In 2006, I'd researched the history of slavery and this led me to the music created by the slaves of Africa. The African slaves in America were captured spirits, torn from their homes and families, oppressed in a foreign land. And from this brooding terrain would rise a beat that would influence and change the musical landscape forever. The music was filled with the pain and anguish expressed, invested, in music as a legacy of their experience. It reached out from the past and touched me in my sorrow.

I searched out spirituals and gospel songs, many remembered from my childhood. I knew the songs already but now it was as though I was hearing them for the first time. I'd remembered the music as joyful, with that infectious rhythm that got everyone swaying and rocking. Now I was hearing a darker mood.

Dorsey's songs led me to F. C. Barnes, Albertina Walker, Cleophus Robinson and others, including that great freedom hymn 'I don't feel no ways tired' by James Cleveland, and particularly 'I stood on the banks of Jordan'.

My friend Bill Hampson organized a tour for the Gospel star Jessy Dixon and asked me to pick him up from London Heathrow and drive him to his first gig.

The road to Birmingham was marked by stories of music and missed turns. Jessy, who died in 2011, left us a legacy of remarkable music but there was one song that reached me as an anthem of personal inspiration: 'We still have work to do.' It was as though he had written the song just for me in my season of desolation, and was saying, come on . . .

Dorsey's music belonged in that genre of old-school gospel, songs that I'd heard as a youth. As I delved further into the music, more songs from my childhood came to mind. Songs my mother played on the piano, songs that we listened to on scratchy 78rpm vinyl records, songs that we heard late at night on the radio, songs I hadn't thought of in decades.

The music I'd listened to before 27 December 2007 remains on the shelf. Perhaps one day I will find the inclination to return there. For now, I'm absorbed by the music that Dorsey invented from the rhythms inspired by the slaves of Africa. The songs took on new meaning and brought comfort. In a way I can't explain, while I was in a cold, unfamiliar place, disconsolate and broken, the music soaked into my subconscious and my spirit and it lifted me. The songs became prayers.

Lord keep me day by day . . . I've been in the storm too long . . . Lead me, guide me . . . Precious Lord, take my hand . . .

# CHAPTER 9

# How to Make Sense of the World?

## *2010*

In April, I found myself at Waterloo Station talking to a young filmmaker who had returned from Uganda with a gruesome story of kidnapping, witchcraft rituals and child sacrifice.

A friend had asked me to meet Kirsty Jones and I had been confident that it wouldn't last longer than a cappuccino at Carluccio's. This wild story had to be one of three things: false, exaggerated or a con. But I found her a credible witness to this shocking crime. I didn't 'feel' like getting involved, but a sense of responsibility pushed me forward.

On the train journey home, I sketched out a strategy. We commissioned Kirsty to return to Uganda to start work on a film that documented the facts. Through Kirsty, we met Peter Sewakiryanga and agreed a partnership with his organization. As always, we only responded if a local group needed help and requested our involvement.

Kirsty's dramatic footage included an interview with a young Ugandan mother and a photograph of her dead child who had been sacrificed. I struggled to finish watching the rough cut. I had approached this as an assignment. It was in Uganda, far removed from my life. Now, I was faced with a mother who endured the same torment: the loss of a child. But her child had died in the most brutal manner.

Several people worked on researching cases of child sacrifice and later my son Luke helped to edit our report. At the same time, we prepared an online petition calling on the Ugandan authorities to protect their children.

Frequently, I felt exhausted, and wondered if I could continue. I recalled a technique picked up at some long-forgotten seminar. In simple terms, it was to break everything down into small parts and tackle one thing at a time. The device worked.

Our campaign focused on the story of Allan, a young boy who had been kidnapped and mutilated as part of a witchcraft ritual. He survived and identified his kidnapper, who lived in the same area. We helped his family move to a new house, some distance away, and later, Allan was taken to Australia for life-saving surgery.

We didn't have funds to pay for the campaign. However, a few months earlier, one of our supporters had remembered Jubilee Campaign in their will. Her gift paid campaign expenses. I wished that I could tell this kind lady the impact her legacy had made.

We decided to promote the campaign in July at New Wine a church conference in Somerset. But first, there was a different event to organize, set for one month earlier.

\* \* \*

Love had bloomed for Rachel and Matt, as did our affection for him. There were two particular occasions when his character shone through.

Rachel was visiting the Rickards when Matt offered to help Craig, who was repairing one of his children's cycles. Later, Craig told us that Matt had fixed the problem without bragging that he'd worked in a bike shop. He didn't need to minimize Craig's efforts in order to demonstrate his skills. He just got on with it.

Earlier that year, Matt approached me one evening and, in the nicest possible way, spoke of his love for Rachel, and his intention to ask her to be his wife. He was, in effect, asking for her hand in marriage. In this brash age of irreverent attitudes, it made us so happy to know that this young man was expressing the noble intention of establishing a home for our daughter, and was going to make her the centrepiece of his life.

One evening, while on holiday in Saint Lucia, Matt led Rachel to an arch, a popular spot for weddings. Enjoying the spectacular view, at sunset, she turned and found Matt on bended knee: he proposed to her.

They set their sights on a June wedding.

Joan and I were delighted but recognized that paying for the reception would be a hurdle to overcome. We agreed on one thing: we wanted to give the couple a day to remember. We scouted around for venues, but every option exceeded our budget. Rachel had her eye on Foxhills, a luxury hotel and spa with three golf courses, all set in a rolling four-hundred-acre estate. It was a perfect venue, but when we did the maths it just confirmed what we already knew: this was completely out of our league, and only feasible if we took out a loan.

Rachel didn't know of our private concerns and her response was typical: 'Let's try it.' A date was set to meet with the wedding planner at Foxhills. I wanted Joan to talk her out of it. 'Don't go there. Don't show her exactly what she can't have.'

I dreaded the visit and stayed home. I assumed the meeting would be over quickly and expected to see them return, with Rachel in tears.

But about two hours passed. Perhaps Joan had given in? It was the loan option. Or Rachel had been so upset, she was being consoled with a double espresso?

When they returned, Rachel was beaming. So was Joan.

The meeting with the wedding planner had gone well until the costs came up. As expected, the fees were astronomical. The wedding planner noticed how dejected Rachel looked, and then asked her, 'How flexible are you about the wedding on Saturday?'

'Flexible!' Rachel shot back. 'Why?'

'Saturday's costs are higher,' she explained. 'But if you change the date from Saturday to Sunday, we can offer you a reduced rate.'

Rachel agreed a Sunday date for the wedding and Joan paid a deposit immediately. The costs were just slightly over our budget, but we were overjoyed that, with the shuffling of dates, we could give Rachel the wedding she'd longed for with the man of her dreams.

Rachel and Matt's wedding was celebrated on 6 June and Reverend Ben Beecroft conducted the service at St Paul's Church in Addlestone. It was a perfect summer's day and I was honoured to walk my daughter down the aisle. The building itself still held strong emotions for me. But it was a wonderful moment fired by an intense poignancy. Rachel was laying down a foundation for the next stage of her life. Her wedding signalled a change in the atmosphere and this act was transforming the memory of a sadness into a celebration.

I had an image of their marriage as a rainbow in the sky – a gift to our family.

Rachel made a radiant bride and the reception at Foxhills was brilliant. Hazel Thompson's gift as photographer guaranteed fantastic images of Rachel and Matt's special day. Matt is an IT wizard who could easily fix almost any computer problem. With that in mind, Joan contributed the best line of my wedding speech. It got the biggest laugh of the night: 'I don't feel like I'm losing a daughter but gaining 24-hour technical support.'

* * *

The following month we set off for New Wine, to publicize our campaign to end child sacrifice in Uganda. As expected, people were shocked by the gruesome subject and many responded. A few months later, Chris Rogers, an investigative journalist, asked us to work with him on a BBC film about child sacrifice. I travelled with Chris in the UK and later we organized the BBC's visit to Uganda to continue the investigation.

Child sacrifice was the lead item on BBC TV News (in October 2011) and Huw Edwards held up our report. We were prominently featured, and the coverage gave a huge boost to our campaign.

The television reports and later a prominent feature on the *Mail Online* website spurred thousands of people in over one hundred countries worldwide to sign our online petition. Later, Chris's BBC documentary, *Uganda – Child Sacrifice*, was nominated for an Emmy, the highest commendation given in television. It was a stunning achievement, and everyone had played a role, particularly our supporter's legacy that paid to kick-start the campaign; without her forethought, kindness and generosity this campaign might never have got started.

\* \* \*

My mother's health had been in decline but deteriorated rapidly during 2010, and she was frequently in hospital. She was frail but determined to witness her granddaughter's wedding in June. A few months after Rachel and Matt's wedding, mum was back in St Peter's Hospital in Chertsey. The doctor warned that she didn't have long, and we visited her daily.

I was getting ready to visit mum in early November when Devaraj phoned. He told me the latest news about the girls from the Jubilee Homes. He referred to the rescued children as 'our sons and daughters', and reminded me that it had been over four years since I was last in India. Devaraj said they were planning an event to mark his organization's twentieth anniversary. 'We want you with us for this special occasion.'

I drove to the hospital with his words ringing in my ears.

When I reached the ward, mum was drowsy from her medication, so I sat quietly beside her bed. She roused, spoke a few words, then drifted back to sleep. I hadn't told her anything about Devaraj's phone call. As I sat by her bedside, I considered a whistle-stop trip. I wondered how many days I'd be away. If I caught a night flight, I'd arrive at midday in Mumbai ...

At that exact moment, mum opened her eyes and looked at me. She said, 'Danny, you're not going anywhere, are you?'

'No, mum,' I replied. 'I'm not going anywhere.'

'Good.' She wriggled her hand, searching for mine. I reached out and stroked her palm. Within minutes, she had drifted back into a light slumber.

That was settled. I phoned Devaraj the next day. I was sorry to let down a good friend, but it was the right decision.

Mum's condition worsened even further. By the second week of November, things looked bleak. Clement was devoted to mum and rarely left her side. 'She's going to get over this,' he insisted. 'She'll come home soon.'

On Friday 12 November, Joan and I returned to the hospital in the morning. Mum was in an eight-person ward on the right-hand side of the room at the far end near the wall. She was asleep but about an hour later, she stirred. She wasn't distressed but there was some inner movement. Joan and I took up a position on either side of her. I stroked her gently. I told her I loved her, and that she would always be my hero. We repeated a few verses from the Shepherd Psalm, her favourite Scripture.

Her breathing increased with some intensity and then eased. There was an audible sound in her throat, and that faded. Joan looked at me. Her eyes said everything that was needed in that moment. My mother, aged 89 years, had lived a good and full life, and her passing was graceful. She looked calm and at peace, as if she was asleep.

We stepped away and drew the curtain around her bed. Joan and I embraced. The others in the ward understood.

Clement wasn't there in that final moment but perhaps it would have been too much for him. We phoned him and he returned immediately. I had never seen him express emotion before, but he looked hopelessly sad as he walked toward mum's bed. After he stepped behind the curtain, we heard him sobbing. My cousin Pam and her children, Melanie and Tim, arrived an hour later. Mum had raised Pam, and they'd been particularly close. Her brother Freddy had been my boyhood hero, and I'd thought of her as my big sister.

Pam was weeping. 'I never knew my mother. She was like a mother to me,' she said through her tears.

Mum had been in pain for the final weeks of her life. Though we were upset, there was also a sense of relief. Everyone who saw her commented on how peaceful she looked.

The death of my mother became part of my life and experience. Yes, I knew about death. It was an indisputable fact, an experience visited on everyone. But when the cold-steel hand of death reached out and touched me personally in December 2007, it revealed one thing: I knew nothing about death.

Death takes you to such a mysterious place. It's a far and distant land, an unknown country, hardly given a second thought, until you are called to journey through it.

\* \* \*

All the messages that we received after December 2007 expressed sympathy and support. Except for one.

The author of this letter told me that the loss I had suffered was punishment from God. It instructed me to seek forgiveness from my Maker. The letter-writer was from a local church and volunteered with Jubilee Action. His letter had factual errors, inevitable when you hear one side of the story. (He'd never asked me about the issues). I replied to him, correcting some inaccuracies, but I couldn't go into details because of the confidentiality agreement I had signed. A second letter arrived, stronger in tone, more forceful in its judgemental condemnation.

I showed the letters to Joan. With her agreement, I tore up the correspondence, and we put it out of our minds.

\* \* \*

I didn't blame God. Neither did I think that God was punishing me. Nor did I harbour feelings of anger or resentment. I'd set down such emotions at the memorial service in January 2008. didn't turn to God in my crisis and find comfort either. I didn't cry out to God to discover that He'd heard my plea and given me hope or taken away my pain. I didn't crawl to God on my knees to find help. The hammer of grief had fallen. I couldn't turn or twist or cry or move or crawl. I was too shocked and crushed and devastated to do anything. Perhaps I was too numb to have any feelings at all. The days didn't get any easier and the feeling of loss never left me.

It was at this lowest point, of breaking, of falling, that I experienced the abiding presence of God. It was a strange contradiction beyond my comprehension: I felt closer to God, more than I ever had before. All this at a time when the compelling power of loss was deepest with the most unimaginable pain bearing down and crushing me.

My spiritual journey had begun when my mother took me to church as a child. I was led to personal faith by George Verwer of OM, as a youth. I acknowledged the spirituality within others though their beliefs might not align exactly with my own, and felt comfortable with those from different streams of the Christian faith. Later in life, I took a holiday from my beliefs, my grip on faith weak. I stopped using religious jargon and the rebel in me took guilty pleasures from teasing others about what I believed or didn't believe.

But I was secure in my faith, however feeble it was. I didn't feel the need to express things in a way that pleased anyone. Faith was woven through my life. It wasn't something to pick up and put down, like shopping in a supermarket. It wasn't a robe to try on to see if it fitted or suited the fashion of the day, or if it made me feel comfortable when I wore it. Faith wasn't something to pick up when life was going well and then discard when it wasn't or when problems arose. Faith wasn't a code of ethics or a top ten list of beliefs to be memorized and signed, like a loyalty card from some superstore. Faith was part of my world, on the good days and the bad days. Faith was experiential, that movement through the day when we encounter the Divine, when we advance through the traffic of life's struggles, the turbulence amidst the delights of everyday pleasures, the fulfilment from achievements, the challenges of changing fortune.

In Steven Spielberg's film, *Minority Report*, Tom Cruise played the role of John Anderton, a detective who tracked killers before they commit their crimes. Why can't life imitate art? I am not the first to question God when things go wrong or disaster strikes. Why can't a supreme ubiquitous all-powerful Being stop the accidents that strike down the innocent? Why does one get plucked to safety, yet another perishes? Are we pawns scrambling in some terrifying games-simulator module where a malignant presence lurks in deep space, smirking as another aeroplane goes down or a river breaks its banks, flooding a village? Or a barren land turns on its people or mothers lose their struggle to protect their children in a refugee camp or border town, with marauding forces closing in for yet another massacre? Why are some treated with apparent random unfairness: a teenager's youth cruelly ravaged by a crippling condition? A devoted Christian father takes early retirement and finds life snubbed out with lung cancer even though he's a non-smoker? Such questions can be tormenting. Simply, are catastrophes (both personal and communal) evidence of the absence of God?

Oh! If only we could devise a Hollywood ending or plot twist to some of life's unfolding sagas. But *Minority Report* was made in Hollywood and its scenario about a 'pre-crimes' department was conjured up by the great science fiction writer Philip K. Dick. Back to earth, the reality is this: catastrophes happen. Innocent children suffer. Ruthless bullies grab power. Terrible things happen in our world, often to the good and the innocent.

The sweep of Scripture records that no one is exempt from the pain of personal anguish. Abraham must have felt the torment as he climbed Mount Moriah with his son, Isaac. Even Jesus shed tears over the loss of a friend.

How suffering exists, occasionally thrives, in a universe ruled by a loving God remains a conundrum. Simplistic or patronising explanation ring hollow. After the lashes of heartbreak, for some, faith fades or changes its shape, while others rise with beliefs that shine. Perhaps it's daring to consider that acts of kindness demonstrate the presence of God amidst the madness of a world aflame. In 'Man in Black', my favourite Johnny Cash song, he reminds us that some things will never be right. That song lyric summed up such complexities better than lofty phrases from theologians and philosophers.

Perhaps the despair I felt didn't fit the script for some people who couldn't understand why I wasn't reporting a supernatural experience that wiped away every tear and moved me on from the paralysis that was grinding me down. But our lives don't always follow straight lines. They twist and turn, like the bend in the river that snakes its way through the city.

Joan attended St Paul's Church, while I joined her irregularly. The church itself still carried stinging memories. Sometimes stepping into the building made me slightly dizzy and I had to steady myself. It reminded me of a journey I had taken as a youth, with my friend Alan Clemence, to the kingdom of Nepal. We boarded a bus before dawn broke, at a small border crossing between India and Nepal. The bus wound its way on that mountain road, stopping so passengers could view the Himalayan range as guides pointed out Mount Everest. As the bus climbed upward, the temperature changed. The air became rarer the higher up we rose, with the risks greater as the driver thrust the vehicle forward, literally at the edge of the cliff. It was the most dangerous journey I'd ever taken, matched by the beauty of the landscape, which was spectacular and unrivalled by anything I'd seen anywhere. Here back on solid ground in Surrey, I was being rocked off balance, still unable to sit on the right-hand side of the church because remembrances of that memorial service in January 2008 stormed back.

People at St Paul's made a big effort, and the vicars, Ben and Chris Beecroft, did everything they could to reach out to us. They invited me to talk about Jubilee Campaign. When I spoke, images and encounters with Jessica darted into my mind, leaving me lost for words, or covering up like a boxer being mauled by Sonny Liston. Memories of Jessica were like the centre of gravity and I was pulled into its vortex. St Paul's had a cracking worship band and the music stirred me. As some members, including the Rickards, moved on, we stayed and new friendships were forged.

St Paul's, under the Beecrofts' leadership, reminded me of a large sprawling oak tree. Its shadow and influence stood tall on the horizon. On one side, it stretched across the M25, London's 117-mile-long orbital motorway, sometimes called London's biggest car park, and on the other, it reached into Addlestone, a bustling town name-checked by HG Wells in *The War of the Worlds*. The church gave us shelter in our moment of sorrow yet welcomed us with music and laughter on joyous occasions, such as Rachel's wedding (and later the baptism of her children). I read somewhere that the oak takes only what it needs from the soil and gives back to the earth, nurturing all nearby.

\*\*\*

People sent me books and articles and personal recollections, and I read each one avidly. Elisabeth Kubler Ross published her definitive work, *On Death and Dying*, in 1997. Though it was instructive, I found her book, written eight years later, *On Grief and Grieving*, with her much-copied thesis of the stages of grief (denial/anger/bargaining/depression/acceptance), particularly helpful. It offered a structure to explain what was happening to me. I started to understand the dynamics of shock and denial in a way that I never had before. It identified that raw, emotional pain of something being wrenched and ripped out from deep within. I recognized my experience in the pages of her book. I didn't want to accept what had happened. I was still in shock, stumbling towards depression. Yet, I couldn't imagine a moment when 'acceptance' would become part of my experience.

I felt I was entering a depression for the first time in my life. This was a state with no exit and no way back because nothing would change. I had lost interest in all the things that used to stir me. I realized this when I spotted a book I had been searching for in a shop near Waterloo Station, but didn't have the inclination to take it from the shelf. I turned away and returned to wait on the platform for the train that would take me home.

There were days when I wondered who would miss me if I wasn't alive. On other days, I questioned the things that required me to get up in the morning. If I had been on my own, I would probably have stayed in bed, unanchored in my own universe. Yet not lost, but just reliving memories of times past.

I loved the moments with Luke and Rachel and Matt when they dropped in. One Monday evening that summer, Luke phoned for a lift after he'd been in London. While driving to Woking, I realized that I had unconsciously arranged to meet him at the same spot from where I'd pick up Jessica. I pictured her standing there, that flicker of recognition and eye contact when she spotted me. And in the car, 'Thanks Dad.' She always turned and looked directly at me. A detail, I only remembered now.

Someone suggested that I took time off: visit Fr Shay in the Philippines or Devaraj in India. Hazel Thompson proposed that our mutual friends donate their unused airmiles for a Smith family holiday. It was a sweet gesture but going away wouldn't solve anything. I had to make sense of the world spinning around me and find my place in it. I didn't know if I could ever reach that destination, but I wasn't troubled by it. This was the way it was going to be from now on.

# CHAPTER 10

# A Message

*2010 – 2013*

Jessica's room was untouched and unchanged. Everything just the way she had it. I liked it when I walked up the stairs to find the door ajar. It gave me the feeling that she was still moving around. That she could appear at any time and call out to me. But I struggled to enter her room. Perhaps I avoided going in because it would confirm what I already knew but couldn't face.

On 9 July, a month after Rachel's wedding, I was alone in the house. I found courage and walked into Jessica's room. I stood by the window. This was her view. This was the place where she stood and looked at the garden below. I looked around. Indy, her cat, had pushed her door open, and was now curled up asleep on her bed. Her shoes and sandals and slippers, all neatly bundled. Her souvenirs, mementos, trinkets, her black and silver top, the tiny hand carved wooden box with drawers. I recognized things I had given her. I spotted one of my books on her shelf.

I noticed an unusual little box on top of her wardrobe and knew immediately that it was mine. She had a way of taking my things. When found out, she'd give me a knowing glance, a hint of a smile – that look. The box was filled with bangles, some loose, others banded together. The bangles took me to the afternoon in India when she purchased them. Her eyes lit up when we were at the stall. The bright, glittery, shiny bangles dazzled and mesmerized her. She wanted to buy the shop. This one. That one. And look at those. She didn't have the heart to bargain with the vendor, though she made a half-hearted attempt. They settled on a price, both smiling. Later, an acquaintance scolded, 'You paid too much. You were cheated.' But Jessica was disinclined to listen. Her empathy was for people scraping a living from such sales.

As I stood there, it came to me that she had chosen everything here and given its place in the room. This simple obvious fact brought me closer to her. I stayed in the room, smiling, looking around again, as particular items reminded me of moments we'd shared. I recalled someone expressing the wish that one day I would remember her with smiles and joy; at the time, I was convinced that it would never happen. That feeling hadn't passed, I can't imagine that I will never be in pain again. But at this moment, I remembered Jessica and smiled.

I collected her photo albums and notebooks. I opened one album and saw a picture of Jessica with a child in her arms in the rural fields of Africa. She looked so happy. How she must have fussed over the child.

The first few photographs were taken during our unforgettable visit to India. The images brought it all back. The kids in Mumbai. The snake charmer with a cobra near the Taj Hotel. The young woman and her child. Reverend Devaraj. Wanno and Roley. The road to the Taj Mahal and the bear tormented by its owner.

I turned the page in the photo album and my eyes fell on something Jessica had written. Then I looked closer at the words:

Dad ...

There it was. A message in Jessica's unmistakable handwriting. To me.

I read and re-read her words. This was different from the captions to photographs in the album. It was her message to me.

I held her photo album close. Something stirred below the surface, like an emotional submarine that crept forward with stealth. An aching giving way to a strange form of peace, this gift from Jessica to me.

\* \* \*

In December, Lord Alton asked me to get involved with the organization former MP Anthony Steen was setting up to deal with trafficking. Years earlier, we had worked with David on an important trafficking initiative but now I didn't think there was anything I could do; equally I couldn't refuse Lord Alton. I was relieved when Mr Steen suggested we met in the new year. To add cover, I asked Bill Hampson of the Epiphany Trust to join me.

As the end of the year drew near, a sadness seemed to descend on our family. This was to be our third Christmas without Jessica. And then more anniversaries.

The day that changed everything. The day she went away. No, that's not right. The day she left. That's not right either. The day she moved from one world to another.

Like most families, Christmas had been a time of celebration for us, but things were different now. For me, Christmas was cancelled. At the same time, her presence remained strong, like some perfume always in the air, always near me. The contradictions were hard to explain,

I awoke in the early hours of Christmas Day, probably around 4am. The room was dark, the stillness of the early morning roused me. I was enveloped in the fading images of a dream. I could see every scene clearly as if broadcast onto a HD widescreen. The dream was portrayed in striking black and white images. Jessica and I were at an event in another country. We were inside a huge wood-lined hall, with windows that looked out on an idyllic countryside. It was winter, the trees were bare, with a light mist in the air. The meeting place was packed, so crowded that I could only see the people around me. I couldn't see Jessica, yet I knew she was in the room. We had arranged to travel on somewhere after the event. I knew the crowd had to thin out before I'd find her. But I was assured I'd see her again. I had to wait.

The dream was a living moment. We were both present in every scene, though not together.

\* \* \*

In January 2011, Bill Hampson and I met Anthony Steen at the Mermaid Theatre Complex near Blackfriars, in a room that overlooked the Thames. It was great having Bill there as this reduced my participation. Together, we developed a plan to mark Anti-Slavery Day. I suggested that annual awards should give special recognition to people and initiatives that had made an impact. Mr Steen liked the idea and Bill and I were tasked with organizing the first awards event which David Alton hosted in the House of Lords (in October) on Anti-Slavery Day.

That same month, I had an appointment at our local health centre. After an earlier blood test, Joan predicted my diagnosis: type 2 diabetes. I walked out of the doctor's surgery with a prescription for metformin.

'How long will I have to take these drugs?' I asked the nurse.

'The rest of your life,' she replied.

Stress was the likely cause of my diabetes.

Joan embarked on a crash-course into responses to diabetes and her day and night research produced several options. We settled on Dr Calvin Ezrin, an endocrinologist, and followed the dietary advice set out in his book *The Type 2 Diabetes Diet Book*. It was tough but I set my mind on my first and only diet. I had surprisingly few cravings and no secret chocolate binges.

Along with this strict regime, we walked a half hour every day. I tested my blood-sugar after every meal, but as it wasn't very high, I never took the drugs. Joan supported me and followed the diet with me. When I returned to the health clinic after three months, my blood sugar readings were normal. The diabetes nurse told me that mine was the most dramatic result they had ever seen.

I came off Dr Ezrin's extreme diet after three months, having evolved new taste buds. I acquired an appetite for green tea, fish, vegetables, nuts, fruit and dark chocolate. I followed a menu low in carbohydrates, high in vegetables, rich in olive oil, similar to a Mediterranean diet, and gradually added a more normal selection of food. Meanwhile, I lost all taste for sugary food and snacks. The diagnosis at my annual check-up, (in 2013), was that my diabetes had been reversed. The disease was now controlled by diet and exercise. Later, I would formally be categorized as 'Diabetes resolved'.

These days, I have the freedom to eat anything but aim to choose wisely. Joan still has the drug prescription that I was originally given as a reminder of how different things could have been.

Sometime during the year, I contracted a throat infection that caused distress when I spoke. A speech therapist at St Peter's Hospital in Chertsey prescribed a series of exercises to strengthen my vocal chords; one was to rest my voice and reduce the times I spoke. I joked that there'd be many people who would be delighted with that instruction. The therapist was brilliant and gave me confidence that things would get back to normal; in all it took a year.

I asked the therapist at one session what had caused my throat infection. She replied, 'It could be a few things; the weather; some lingering infection; or stress. Have you been stressed recently?'

I'd never thought of stress as an illness with physical symptoms. Previously, when someone said they were suffering from stress, I was tempted to tell them: 'Get real. Think of someone with a real problem.' Until it happened to me, I found it difficult to sympathize or comprehend what others were going through. But I was wrong. For me, I needed a physical reminder. And it wasn't long before I got it.

One afternoon that summer, Joan and I drove to Walton, a town on the River Thames, about six and a half miles from our home. Walton had been one of our regular jaunts when the children were young. I parked on a cul-de-sac off Terrace Road on the A3050 and we set off towards Walton Bridge in the direction of the high street. We browsed in a second-hand furniture shop, and another selling mirrors. We stepped outside and continued towards the high street.

Suddenly, I was lying on the pavement and there were cars whizzing by. I heard Joan's soothing voice in my ear. A man rushed over. I heard the end of his sentence to Joan, '... phone for an ambulance, love?'

I couldn't understand what had happened. Why was I lying on the pavement? Who needed an ambulance?

Joan helped me up and dusted me down. I insisted we carry on to the street and quizzed her about the missing few seconds. She told me I had suddenly turned away and headed into the street. And then I collapsed. I didn't have any explanation. Neither did I have a memory of fainting, though my bruised hands and knuckles were all the evidence I needed as proof. But it was a physical act. It made me acknowledge that I had a problem, and that I was suffering from a real disease: stress.

I think naming it helped. It was the start of a journey back to health, physical, at least.

\* \* \*

On 3 August 2011, Seth Newman was born. I didn't realize it at the time, but Matt and Rachel's first child would start to lift the sorrow that had been like a shadow over our family for the last four years.

Seth developed an attachment to Joan and took to carrying a photograph of his grandmother. Over time, the paper photograph crumpled but was replaced with a laminated image that put its indestructability to the test. In his own way, this child who couldn't yet speak had started to bind together the family.

Luke developed a natural affection for Seth and became his favourite uncle. Six months later, Luke had a big surprise of his own, when his daughter Lily Grace was born. Once more, the birth of a child played an influential role in our lives.

Lily's birth was to have a profound effect on Luke. The past few years hadn't been easy, but he had overcome his own personal issues with fortitude and determination. Still, we wondered what pathway would open up for him. He turned to his childhood passion and enrolled in a Computer Games Design course at the University of Westminster. But nothing could have prepared us for the way he responded when his former partner, Holly, broke the bombshell news that he was a father. He told us, 'This will be the making of me.'

He matched his words with deeds and never looked back. Holly and Luke shared custody and worked the arrangements with maturity. He took on the responsibility of being a single parent and dedicated himself to putting Lily first, setting that as the measure for every decision he made. It can't have been easy, but he developed new skills, faced challenges head-on, and grew in maturity, as his adoration for his child shone through in everything he did. All this while in his final term at university. Over that season, Joan and I watched our son turn from a youth into a man. We were inspired by the remarkable transformation that a child had ignited in him.

Lily's exuberance for life was matched by her confidence. Joan's little red car converted into 'Nan's Taxi' as grandmother and granddaughter bonded.

* * *

I didn't know if I could take Jubilee Campaign forward or how we'd face the future. A friend expressed dismay on hearing that we intended to rebuild Jubilee Campaign. 'Don't do it,' he cautioned.

Our first concern was that we didn't have money to pay for operating costs for the girls at the Jubilee Homes. In the past, we'd relied on the generosity of our 25,000 strong database. Now, we had too few people to reach our target. But I held close to Joan's affirmation of love and her prophetic word about Gideon over our calling and mission. I believed that God delivers help when we need it. I had seen His provision many times. Still, in that moment, fear was high, faith low.

The first breakthrough came from Olivia Harrison. She directed over $200,000 from the George Harrison Fund for UNICEF to the work in India. She hadn't forgotten us, and it carried the Jubilee Homes for a few years. Billy Connolly's manager Steve Brown tried to cheer us. He offered a holiday, among other things. When Billy announced a new tour in 2009, they added a charity night, and gave the entire evening's proceeds to Jubilee Campaign.

Both Olivia and Billy had donated hundreds of thousands of pounds over the years. But those specific gifts reached us when we needed them most. For a few years after that, support from Hard Rock Cafe filled the gap. Later, with pressure mounting, donations from the Exodun Trust surprised us with faithful regularity. We believed the timing of these particular donations fulfilled Joan's prophetic word. It meant we could keep our commitments.

Joan's role with the night nursing service at St Peter's Hospital ended after two years and she took up a fulltime job with us. The work grew slowly, as did our mailing list. Our supporters were like a small community of friends. They knew us, understood our struggles, prayed for us (some daily), wrote heart-warming messages, and phoned occasionally. Their loyalty and generosity were humbling. I wish I could name each one here.

In December 2012, we wrote to everyone about an important new programme that had started in the Philippines through the kindness of our friend, Fr Shay Cullen: The Jessica Smith Scholarship Fund.

At Jessica's memorial service, we had told friends about our plans to set up charitable tributes in her name. We wanted to remember Jessica by celebrating her life and decided this was best accomplished through the narrative of helping others. George Verwer was the first to respond with a cheque of £1,000. Our friends were generous; one wrote, 'I hope that this will bring you some comfort.'

We decided that the tributes should be in countries which Jessica had visited or had intended to visit, and settled on India, the Philippines and Zimbabwe. When I mentioned the idea to Fr Shay, he suggested a scholarship fund for children at risk of being trafficked. He emailed:

> It seems only yesterday that we were together. That last meal together is frozen in time for me. This is a beautiful way to remember Jessie, something that will live on and on . . . giving new life to the impoverished is best done this way, as whole lives, families and generations are best influenced through education, especially for young girls.

Fr Shay had taken the aspirations that were unformed in our hearts and spoken life to them. It was humbling to learn that the first donation was a personal gift of 3,000 euros from Fr Shay himself. He promoted the scholarship fund and told us that it was doing well with no dropouts. 'I look on them as Jessie's kids. This is what she would have been doing. Working in the developing world. Giving life into the future for kids that would otherwise end up on the dumpsite of humanity. Now they have a bright future – and their children also.'

We circulated Fr Shay's article to our small band of supporters, and many responded. I answered everyone personally; my wrist ached from the number of letters I wrote daily, yet I was grateful for each response.

\* \* \*

Rachel and Matt's second child, a daughter, was born at quarter past midnight on a snowy night on 4 April 2013.

Rachel felt a closeness with Jessica that night. She had arranged a home birth and the midwife was accompanied by a young trainee. Rachel recognized her immediately. It was Louise, one of Jessica's classmates, who had been a regular visitor to our home. The poignancy of the encounter increased when Louise told Rachel that she had finished her training as a midwife, but this was her first assignment.

Joan's role that night (to her delight) was to care for two-year old Seth in our home, his first sleepover; together, grandparents and grandson returned the morning after the main event. Rachel and Matt bore their weariness with the joy that the birth of a child brings. I knew that feeling and recognized it in the way that they moved with each other.

During our visit, someone placed the tiny 6lb 10oz child in my arms. My mind was immediately drawn to twenty-eight years ago, when I had first held a just-born baby. Within minutes, I felt comfortable cradling this precious new creation in my arms.

Rachel arranged for her daughter to be baptized at St Paul's. The church was packed with family and friends, who had come to share this special occasion with our family. When I stepped inside the church, I felt the old emotions crowding in, and remembered the first time I walked into the same building for a very different service in 2008. I pushed myself towards Joan in the second row. It seemed a long walk to cross the floor of the sanctuary to reach her.

When it was time for the baptism, Ben asked Rachel and Matt, 'What name do you wish this child to be baptized with?'

'Eden Jessica,' Rachel replied.

I caught my breath as I heard the name of Jessica called aloud in the church.

The birth of a child is usually an occasion of great joy. And that's how it was with the arrival of our grandchildren, Seth and Lily. Now with Eden, I believed the promise that they were gifts from God to lift our hearts.

* * *

A few months after Eden's birth, Lord Alton told me, 'Wonderful news. I've invited Chen Guangcheng to visit the UK.'

'That's brilliant,' I agreed. We'd campaigned for the release of the blind barefoot lawyer imprisoned in China for defending the rights of women and the disabled. David whizzed through a proposed itinerary: an awards ceremony in Parliament; the Oxford Union wanted him to address the prestigious group; the list ran and ran. At some point in the conversation, I heard my name mentioned. Would I handle the media?

I had worked in the media and organized numerous press events for past campaigns and was proud of the coverage we'd secured for a group our size. But this seemed like an insurmountable task. I contacted Bill Hampson who was also involved in Mr Chen's visit. He was encouraging but said he wasn't taking this on. It was up to me.

The next twenty-four hours were tense. At first, I put it out of my mind. Then, I listed the reasons why I couldn't take up a task that previously I would have relished. I considered other people to recommend. Eventually, I decided to address the problem and speak to David.

If I gave up now, perhaps it was time to write my resignation. Had this assignment taken me to that point in my life? If so, I should do it on my terms and own the moment. I was scared. Scared that I would fail if I went ahead. Scared that I would end my 'mission' not going forward with something I believed at one point, I had been 'called' to do.

I prayed. Lord, help me. What should I do? It was hardly a prayer, rather a last gasp of weary breath.

I hadn't expected to look out of the window and find sky writing that blazed the answer across the horizon: Danny, I want you to . . . I've had the conviction that God guided me at important points and crossroads in my life. But I'd never been one to lay in bed and pray: Lord, should I get out of bed? Give me a sign.

Praying to know God's will was obviously right, but I've been cautious of advice that expected guidance to function like a GPS satellite navigational system: 'Take the second left' or 'Turn around and make a U turn.' I believed I should take one day at a time and respond to the steps in front of me. There have been occasions when I've instinctively known what to do. At other times, I've detailed the case for and against the choice and this has informed my decision. God gave me a mind to use and free will to choose. But at that moment, such instinctiveness failed me.

I put off calling David until the last possible moment. I didn't want to phone him first thing. Why start his day off with a problem? At midday, I decided the time wasn't right. A headache before lunch could give him indigestion. By early afternoon, a few ideas came to me.

I reflected on the key points of the Chinese dissident's story. His determination to overcome what others considered a disability. His refusal to play the victim. His courage in standing up to the powerful state and fighting for justice for the powerless. His willingness to endure physical hardship for his beliefs.

I compared this to my own feelings of fear, inadequacy and exhaustion. But organizing a media campaign seemed like a high tower, all-powerful and inaccessible.

The first step. The words came into my mind. Take the first step.

I took the first step. I sketched out a media wish-list.

The voice in my head said, 'Start at the top.'

I phoned Chris Rogers, at the BBC. He'd just finished presenting the news.

'Chris, do you remember Chen Guangcheng from . . .'

'China,' he finished the sentence. 'Is there anyone who doesn't know him? He's made headlines around the world.'

'He's coming to Britain,' I said. 'Do you want to interview him?'

I gave Chris the dates. There was a pause on the line. He said, 'No. I'm away.'

Chris probably caught my disappointment across the airwaves. Before, I could reply, he said, 'Leave it with me. I'll find out if the BBC are interested.'

The call bolstered me. I contacted another friend who gave me the number of the head of news at Channel 4 Television. This time, the response was different.

'Yes, absolutely. We want him.'

I told the TV executive that I had approached the BBC, 'How firm is the offer from Channel 4?'

'Oh, it's firm,' he said, with a whiff of annoyance. 'It'll be a main news item – unless there's a political scandal or a celebrity break-up. But if you go with the BBC, the interview is off. How soon can you confirm?'

I assessed the options. Should I accept the offer on the table from Channel 4? Would the BBC even take the story? Before I could conjure up any more things to worry about, my phone rang. It was Chris.

'The BBC are hot for the interview. Call them now.' He rattled off a name and number. 'Got to run.'

I felt drained of energy, but within an hour, the questions I had posed about my future had been answered. We finalized the itinerary a few days later. The BBC wanted Mr Chen for the entire morning. When I grumbled, they listed the programmes that would run his interview. It was worth the investment of time as we'd get global coverage.

I phoned the Channel 4 executive and explained why we had chosen the BBC. He was gracious and understanding. An hour later, he called back.

'We really want Mr Chen,' he said. 'Give me something.'

We kicked around some ideas. Then he said, 'Can we call it his first feature television interview in London?'

'Sure,' I replied.

When I circulated the final media schedule to David, I was stunned with the results. We got everyone we wanted and couldn't fit in all the requests.

Bill asked me to pick up Mr and Mrs Chen from London St Pancras as they were coming in on the Eurostar after meetings in the European Parliament. Although I wanted to meet the Chens, I was apprehensive; I didn't know how to explain the contradictions within.

The renovations to St Pancras had been completed in November 2007 and it looked fantastic. I saw the rush of people coming through and spotted Bob Fu, who served as their translator. I had last seen Bob and Heidy Fu in Hong Kong in 1997. Bob had been a student activist in the Tiananmen Square protests but found faith and worked with China's underground church. They had escaped from China and were hiding out in Hong Kong but feared arrest after Britain handed back the colony, once known as Pirate Island, to the Communist state on 30 June 1997.

I'd flown to Hong Kong to help this young Christian family before the deadline but became embroiled in a complex political tussle. David's lobbying helped and with strategic back-room manoeuvres, they flew out 48 hours before the handover. They settled in Texas and established China Aid to help persecuted believers. Bob was generous about our support in his best-selling memoir, *God's Secret Agent*.

The Chens greeted me like old friends. Bob said, 'I was telling them about you and the last time we met in Hong Kong.'

Guangcheng gripped my arm and gently pushed us forward. He walked with extraordinary confidence and just seemed to know where to go, with a few adjustments from me to avoid a collision. His wife Wei Jing followed with Bob, as we headed to the car park.

Bill had been warned about security concerns over the Chinese dissidents' visit and cautioned us to be alert and discreet. I'd envisaged a secluded corner in a hideaway hotel closeted in some rural backwater. All very hush-hush. But Guangcheng didn't agree with my suggestions for a quiet evening behind closed doors. 'I like to walk,' he said. 'Let's go to Chinatown.'

He was recognized in Chinatown – and everywhere we went. Some came to shake his hand; others wanted a selfie. The Chens wanted food from a particular region, and after settling into their chosen restaurant, Guangcheng said, 'Tell me about yourself.'

The itinerary was packed, and the interviews well received. We'd crammed in a final press conference for South Asian correspondents because their broadcasts reached across China. The *Economist* pushed to change the time of their interview so that the editor could shake his hand. The *Daily Mail* journalist was agitated. He said he'd fit in with any time any place. When we met, the reason became clear. He'd been in China when Guangcheng was taken from Beijing's American Embassy to the hospital for treatment on his broken foot. The correspondent had tried to enter the hospital, but the police threw him out.

On their last day, Joan and I drove Guangcheng and Wei Jing to Heathrow Airport for their flight to New

York City. It had been an action-packed visit. I was drawn to the Chens' warmth and sincerity in our few days together. Even though our language was limited, we connected strongly.

Beyond that, their visit reawakened something dormant within me in recent years. It was a reminder of why I felt called to this mission. Working on the 'media blitz', as someone described it, evoked the imprint of Jessy Dixon's song 'Work To Do'. I heard it calling me. There was still a place for me. And yet I could have missed it.

About the same time, I was in London for another meeting.

I'd helped Hazel Thompson for a few years on a digital photographic project she'd envisioned. 'Taken: Exposing Sex Trafficking and Slavery in India' was launched in October 2013 at a dazzling event hosted by the Hard Rock Cafe in London. Hazel kindly donated the profits to the work. She deserved the recognition she received for her inventiveness and use of ground-breaking technology to complete the e-book.

Meanwhile, my son Luke added his own innovative skills to the project. He produced the Taken Campaign app, using Hazel's powerful images and videos, and included an online petition inspiring people to take action. It was probably the first campaigning app of its kind and was released to mark Anti-Slavery Day at an event hosted by Lord Alton and Fiona Bruce MP, who declared, 'This is the first time a human rights app has been launched in the House of Commons.'

I saw this as a stunning personal achievement, a milestone in his life. Luke continued as a professional freelancer drawing glowing endorsements from clients for his contribution to apps, virtual reality and other digital media; while helping us out when we needed it. He could have launched his own digital agency and life would have been easier. Instead, he only took on assignments that ensured he had enough time to care for Lily. She became the criteria for everything he did. Luke was defined by such decisions. We couldn't have been prouder of our son.

Hazel's ebook attracted wide attention and caught the eye of Canon J. John. His support was an encouragement to Hazel. Later, he suggested I meet his friends, Robin Hay and Meg Duncan, because of our shared interest in justice issues.

I couldn't think of a good enough reason not to meet them. It was the same tension that made me flinch at meeting Chen Guangcheng. I had shut down part of myself and struggled to explain my internal turmoil.

I had a range of masks to conceal the deeper part of myself. I was considering which disguise to present as I found myself at Pizza Express near Trafalgar Square. Robin Hay had flown down from Aberdeen for appointments in London and I was his one o'clock. It was to be the first of several cappuccinos together; later he introduced me to Mrs Meg Duncan.

Robin had a way of drawing me in, while Meg spoke movingly as she told me her own story. Her daughter was dying of a brain tumour yet both mother and daughter shared an inner strength drawn from their personal beliefs. It was evidence of the difference that faith makes to life when confronted with the crisis and calamity some people are called to face. I felt privileged to be part of that intimacy.

Robin and Meg asked about our campaigns, and those were easy questions. But as we got to know each other, I found myself talking about Jessica. It was difficult, and emotional, and on the train back, I wondered what they thought of me. Over time, I spoke more with them about my journey of grief. Perhaps their sensitivity created a safe space that enabled me to share this hidden part of myself.

The meetings helped me realize that I had to reconstruct my life in a way that enabled Jessica to become part of my identity. The journey wouldn't be swift, and the road was long, but I had taken the first step. I'd read about a lady who spoke of the most courageous thing she'd done in her life. When asked how many children she had, her reply was, 'Two. But one had passed.' These encounters (with the Chens, Robin and Meg) had been my moment of courage.

CHAPTER 11

# The Fingerprints of Grief

*2013*

I continued to read everything that came my way about how people dealt with bereavement. There were emails, books, magazine articles, memoirs, pamphlets, self-published accounts, some just a few pages, others downloaded from websites and blogs. Many came from friends and acquaintances, others from strangers who'd heard about us. Jubilee supporters shared their own private experiences. I learned how people worked through adversity and went forward with some form of resolution. Others were consumed, torn by the trauma, their days overtaken by bitterness and guilt, even revenge. Some just couldn't abide what had happened, turned away, unanchored in the tides of distress.

I became aware of this brooding landscape where the lost and the sorrowing took up their post and held high their personal torch of remembrance.

After the actor Paul Newman's son died of a drug overdose, he said everything in his life changed. Ray

Davies of the Kinks didn't speak for a year after the death of his sister Rene (following a heart attack on the Lyceum ballroom dance floor) in 1957. Barry Gee (of the Bee Gees) told *Time Magazine* that after he lost his brothers, 'I just sat around for a long time. You never get past that.' Dido sang 'Raglan Road' to her father as he lay dying; later, she wrote 'Grafton Street'. I tried to imagine how she felt when writing it. Gloria Hunniford spoke of the loss of her daughter, Caron Keating: she said people told her that she 'really should have moved on by now'. But she questioned where she should go. 'I'll never be the person I was: carefree, with everything in its place. All I can do is carry Caron's spirit forwards and try to make sense of something that makes no sense at all.' I'd met the couple and noticed how close mother and daughter had appeared. I remembered them walking out of the room arm in arm laughing, as good friends do.

One person told me I should move on. Another said, 'You don't want to move on, you want to stay this way.' Someone else gave me the name of an 'excellent' counsellor. A woman who'd lost her child years ago expressed surprise when I told her that three years had passed. 'That's nothing,' she said. 'Give yourself time.' One man told me that he had never dreamt about his departed son, as did another. One said they couldn't have a photograph of their child on display in their home.

After her son, Jamie, died of anorexia, aged 25, Anne Shaw-Kennedy, one of our supporters, produced a book of his photographs. The book encapsulated both her love and her loss. Her affection seemed to be embedded in every page. The publication was probably her moment of healing. A friend entrusted me with an intimate glimpse into the world of her child, who lived precariously between life and death, the result of a life-threatening condition. 'She's ready for heaven, it's become a reality to her.' Her daughter lived for the moment when she passed from this world into the next. Another friend emailed me and said, 'I have started to pray for my own funeral. Trusting it will go well. It won't be long now.'

I'd known Dr George Hobbs since the eighties. He was a leader at St Peter's Church in Chertsey, and we'd visited his lovely home when our children were young. George endured the anguish of his son's suicide (in June 2010). The torment of this incident must have been unbearable, but when he wrote to me, this leapt off the page: 'All the memories are good.'

Anne Coombs, from St Paul's, said 'a pain pierced my heart' when she read about Jessica. 'I know what it's like to lose a child. There is no pain like it.'

Olivia Harrison told me, 'This is the time only God and faith can get you through. I know this first-hand. There are no platitudes that will help you but the grace of God is all that can get you through it.'

Steve Brown wrote: 'You spoke of Jess many times when we met in London and I can only imagine the pain that you are suffering at the moment. My brother died at an early age and I saw how difficult it was for my parents to come to terms with the unnatural event of one of their children dying before they did. My heart goes out to you and your family – I just hope that your Christian beliefs are of some comfort at this time.'

It was humbling to be offered glimpses into such intimacy. We felt upheld when people said they were praying for us.

Yuri Belov had served 15 years as a prisoner of conscience in the Soviet Union. Together we'd visited the poet, Irina Ratushinskaya, following her release (in 1986) from the Gulag. Irina and Belov spoke in Russian. On the journey back, Yuri interpreted the exchange: 'She felt the prayers of people in prison. She spoke of something physical. I knew what she meant. I felt it also. Some kind of physical presence, a warmth, outside the normal. Something spiritual. But hard to understand.'

When al-Qaeda attacked America in 2001, 2753 people perished in Manhattan. In *The Eleventh Day*, Anthony Summers said, 'Almost 60% vanished entirely from the earth without leaving even so much as a DNA trace.' The worst terrorist act on US soil generated books, articles, investigations, films, including an Academy award-winning documentary by our friend, the filmmaker Scott Hillier. *Newsweek* magazine's ten-year anniversary edition reminded me of that September day with Jessica in London. The article concluded: New York will never get over it. We move forward but it stays with us.

For me, these words resonated: We move forward but it stays with us. It was the best expression of how I felt.

\* \* \*

Although I read about the grief of others, I considered my loss as distinct from everyone else. I didn't think anyone could have experienced grief with the same intensity.

Everything before 27 December 2007 belonged in a galaxy far, far away, separated from the world I lived in now. That day, that Thursday, was a line in the sand. The day that changed everything when everything changed. The shock of that December day was the enduring sensation that stayed with me. It held the power to start a hurricane in my heart. I struggled to find words to express how I felt. I couldn't recognize this new world that swirled around me, or who I was or where I was going. I no longer had that sense of wonder at the world, with no interest in exploring its hidden pathways or lost highways.

The dictionary defines grief as a noun: intense sorrow, caused by someone's death.

But grief can't be explained. It has to be experienced. Grief is not a puzzle to be solved, a riddle to unravel. Grief lurks suspended and mysterious like an undiscovered continent of our spirit – until you journey through it. And without realising or wanting it, I had set course on a voyage of exploration.

Grief is like our fingerprints, unique to us as individuals. For each one, the process of mourning unfolds differently and sets its own timeline. For some it is a marathon, others a sprint.

Grief is like a language, a secret and hidden form of communication, that lays dormant, buried deep within. It connects us to people with an invisible bond.

Grief transcends religions, reaches across borders, travels beyond countries, enters uninvited and unexpectedly into inner rooms in our homes, exposes things once hidden, recognises no authority or chain of command,

and for some, surprises us like an unexpected knock on the door. For others, it encroaches on our existence like a creeping fog. In the mist it is mystifying, in the dazzling sunlight it is blinding, and frequently leaves us disorientated and confused. It was at once as exhausting as it is transformative.

I didn't know I had the unwanted gift of this language of grief until the moment of its epiphany. And in that instant flash of discovery when it was uncovered, this dialect of heartbreak became alive within me. It spoke to the deep inner part of myself.

Death lives all around – an indisputable fact. When it reached out and touched me, it turned from an academic piece of data into a living flame. It was fire in my hand. It was a sound I'd never heard before.

Winter brought with it more than a change in the weather. Christmas, anniversaries and special occasions carry a dread for some mourners. But not for me. I bear that constantly; every time a familiar song is heard, it taunts me with a jolt from the past, and these tears become a badge.

I heard Joan speak of 'a long winter' and a 'winter season' and understood that she meant more than the season of ninety days or so. A few days later, a friend wrote, 'I thank God for the roses in winter.' Those words evoked the biting cold and howling winds of winter, but also a patch of earth where spirits are renewed. The roses come in various guises: in messages, in words, in song, in Scripture, in thoughts, in a kind deed, in the sensitive embrace of a friend's touch, in a smile, in a look, just one look.

And darkness accompanied the winter season.

I recalled Chen Guangcheng, who took my arm and then advanced like a triumphant conqueror through the crowded terminal at St Pancras. I read about his incredible escape from house arrest in his autobiography (*The Barefoot Lawyer*, described by actor Christian Bale as insanely inspiring), when he evaded his guards – in daylight. Darkness was his secret weapon, a friend joked. Later the celebrated artist Ai Weiwei tweeted: 'You know, he's blind so the night to him is nothing.'

The Episcopalian theologian Barbara Brown Taylor asserted that winter and darkness aren't a sign that God has withdrawn from us, neither is it a chart of our faith level. I knew that church emphasized the joy that faith brings, but it wasn't my present experience. While the accent on joy was uplifting, I was being shown that darkness wasn't to be dismissed or devalued.

Mrs Brown Taylor asserted: darkness was the context for God's interaction with man. God appeared to Abraham in the night with the promise to make his descendants more numerous than the stars. The flight from Egypt in that mighty exodus happened at night. Moses was in the thick darkness on Mount Sinai when God encountered him and handed down the Ten Commandments. When Saul was on the road to Damascus, he lost his sight. That must have been a terrifying experience, but it led to his conversion. The birth of Jesus occurred under a star, his resurrection in the darkness of a cave.

The New Testament is a collection of 27 books, with 13 written by the apostle Paul. His letter to the believers in Philippi in Greece was written while he was in custody awaiting trial in Rome. Paul's letter didn't focus on his physical hardships. Instead, joy is a constant theme.

Paul's dramatic transformation happened when he was blinded on the road to Damascus and heard the voice of God. In our modern world, effective church leadership sometimes relies on inspiring oratory, or skilled marketing or innovative church planting schemes, all good and necessary components for success. Here's the profile offered up by the apostle himself (2 Corinthians 11:23–27: *The Phillips New Testament in Modern English*):

I have served (more) prison sentences! I have been beaten times without number. I have faced death again and again.

I have been beaten the regulation thirty-nine stripes by the Jews five times.

I have been beaten with rods three times. I have been stoned once. I have been shipwrecked three times. I have been twenty-four hours in the open sea.

In my travels I have been in constant danger from rivers and floods, from bandits, from my own countrymen, and from pagans. I have faced danger in city streets, danger in the desert, danger on the high seas, danger among false Christians. I have known exhaustion, pain, long vigils, hunger and thirst, going without meals, cold and lack of clothing.

Scripture records the plots to kill Paul and the persecution he faced throughout his ministry. The apostle was stoned and left for dead in Lystra (Acts 14:19); beaten and imprisoned in Philippi (Acts 16:23). In 2 Corinthians 6:3-10 (New Living Translation), Paul wrote:

> We patiently endure troubles and hardships and calamities of every kind. We have been beaten, been put in prison, faced angry mobs, worked to exhaustion, endured sleepless nights, and gone without food. We prove ourselves by our purity, our understanding, our patience, our kindness, by the Holy Spirit within us, and by our sincere love. We faithfully preach the truth. God's power is working in us. We use the weapons of righteousness in the right hand for attack and the left hand for defence. We serve God whether people honour us or despise us, whether they slander us or praise us. We are honest, but they call us impostors. We are ignored, even though we are well known. We live close to death, but we are still alive. We have been beaten, but we have not been killed. Our hearts ache, but we always have joy. We are poor, but we give spiritual riches to others. We own nothing, and yet we have everything.

\* \* \*

I'd read such Scriptures and through our advocacy work, I was privileged to become friends with people of faith who had suffered for their beliefs and ideas with sacrifices I couldn't imagine. It was such relationships and encounters that had enriched and scorched my life, affirmed my 'calling' and driven me to continue working with Jubilee Campaign.

But things had come easily to me, and such suffering was beyond my own experience. Neither was it a pathway I would choose. It took a while to make a connection between physical suffering and emotional and mental anguish, along with the role – if any – that faith played at times like these. My mind felt empty and barren like a wasteland, as though everything had been wiped. Occasionally, an encounter from the past broke through.

In 1989, we had started a campaign to help the persecuted Christians minority in Nepal and David Alton launched our report on the situation in Parliament. Charles Mendies helped compile the material but was arrested a few months later in Kathmandu. I felt partly responsible and flew to the world's only Hindu kingdom to offer support to his family. I'll never forget the moments with Charles as he spoke to us from behind prison walls, or trips with his wife Susan to visit jailed Nepalese Christians and to a church that had been attacked.

In that same year, Lin Xiangao (Samuel Lamb) had invited us to his home in China. A poster on his front door announced his house arrest and forbade contact. But the house church leader was fearless. Pastor Lamb had already served 20 years in jail. He took us to a room where he led worship. It was in disarray with broken chairs, overturned tables, books strewn around, the result of a police raid. 'What more can they do to us? We trust a greater power,' he said, his voice strong. Before we left, Pastor Lamb asked me to take a photograph of him with the banned poster on his front door. His house was under surveillance so there would only be time for one photograph. No second chances.

And that's what happened. I walked out the door. Took four or five steps into the street. Turned. Raised my camera and pressed the button. Pastor Lamb's face peered out behind the door. The poster was in view. It took a single movement and was completed in seconds.

I glimpsed the depth of faith and richness of spirit of Charles in prison in Nepal and Pastor Lamb under house arrest in China – among others.

When visiting Sweden, I spoke of these experiences with the head of an NGO that supported persecuted Christians. He then told me of an occasion when he had been covertly distributing Bibles in China but still had one copy of the banned book. On his last night, there was a knock on his hotel door. A Chinese man stood in the hallway and said, 'Do you have something for me?'

The unexpected guest had taken a risk entering the hotel. He received the Bible like a jewel

'How did you find me?' my friend asked.

The Chinese Christian said that God had given him a conviction that there was someone in the hotel who had a gift for him. My friend persisted. 'But how did you find me?'

The man said he'd stopped in front of every room and prayed. Then moved on to the next room. He said, 'When I came to your door, I believed this was where God wanted me to be.'

This story came to my mind in 2012, along with flashbacks from visits to Nepal and China. I knew the presence of God, but the sorrow within me was overwhelming. I struggled with the restless tension of both feelings. The reconciliation I reached during this season of grief was this: to find a natural pace and be comfortable with who I am.

Elizabeth Kubler Ross spoke of acceptance for the loss suffered. I hadn't reached that point and didn't know if I ever would, but it didn't trouble me. I wrote in my journal:

> I just know what I know. I know that God is holding me. I know that God will never let me fall. I know that this is the hardest place, the toughest time, the defining moment.

I had always considered myself a strong person, not often needing the support of others, an island self-contained and independent, regardless of what John Donne wrote in his famous poem.

But the loss of Jessica left me devastated and crushed.

Sometimes, I felt like someone who had drifted out to sea and was now stranded on a desert island in the midst of a hidden ocean. At other times, I felt dislocated and adrift from the world I used to know, not lost but separated. I was watching from a rooftop or a high hill far away. News came in from far-off lands, but the events reported were remote and removed from where I was.

I had been hit with a blow so hard that there was nothing in the world left for me, or so it seemed, and nothing that anyone could do would make a difference. Faith remained present, brought sense and calm, and became the glue that held me together. But the emotions tricked me, tripped me up.

Joan and I watched the TV series *The West Wing*. In an episode, one of the characters explained that the key to dealing with trauma was to remember the past without reliving it. The screenwriter Aaron Sorkin's words touched a nerve. It went to the issue that hit me hardest: memories.

I kept replaying the past. Jessica's loss became an incomparable unimaginable weight. I had no future because there was an absence that would never be filled, and no words to describe someone I could never replace. I just wanted to cling on to every part of her memory and never let go. Holding the past was a way of holding on to myself.

I wanted to keep things the way they were. I thought this brought me closer to her, closer to the time when she was with me, by my side. I kept everything I could find that belonged to Jessica. All her books, and magazines, that particular copy of American *Vogue*. I kept the hangers from Bay Trading, the fashion retail shop where she worked during the holidays. Even the curtains that she made for the windows in the box room. They were torn, probably beyond repair. But I didn't want them mended. I wanted everything unchanged, just the way it was, when she was here.

An overseas acquaintance who I'd never met, emailed: 'I was under the impression it was recently, yet for you it'll always seem like it happened recently.'

Memory remains at the heart of human experience, our constant companion on this journey through life. It is such an extraordinary gift to us. In one sense, it's all we've got.

I closed my eyes and surrendered to memory.

Memories came from nowhere. Days. Moments.

That phone call when her car ran out of petrol on the way to a waitressing job. That look when she saw me arrive with a jerry-can of petrol.

That look of surprised joy, when the great jazz singer Lianne Carroll and the Peter Kirtley Band invited us as their guests to Ronnie Scott's Jazz Club, and dedicated a song to her.

The way her long black hair cascaded down her back, the swishing noise it made when she moved forcefully, like the lash of a whip slicing the air behind her.

I found the winter gloves that Jessica gave me, her birthday gift, that last December. She had spoken to me and chuckled in that old familiar way.

Out of nowhere came a memory of that pet shop in Clandon. The children were young. Jessica had stopped at every cage, every cubicle. There was a pond near the entrance. Jessica, Rachel and Luke were all hunched at the edge peering at the fish darting back and forth. I crept up behind Jessica and pretended to push her in but caught her at the last moment. She was mad. Furious. Then she wanted me to do it again. And again. And again.

One evening in December 2007, Jessica had suggested we went for a drive. We cruised local haunts and about an hour later found ourselves in Clandon. We followed the winding path from the main road but before we reached the pet shop, a movement in the distance caught our eye: a muster of peacocks. We stopped the car nearby. It was late in the evening, just around sunset.

No words said, no words needed. Just a moment shared between father and daughter.

That bridge in Ripley . . . I returned and caressed the stones, cold to the touch. That special feeling lives again in my heart.

Such drops of memories pour down on me, cut me, wounds that are seared deep into my consciousness. The tiny flashes, almost forgotten, fragments of time, do the most damage. Moments – of significance to no one but myself. That 'cross' look that she and I recreated. I'd give her a little hug, touch her shoulder or her arm. No words but a silent expression of love. And that slight turn of her head, just the way she looked at me . . . The special way she smiled. That twinkle. That knowing glance.

Somewhere in the depths of my mind a silent voice rings out: this is what life will be. Someone who's had their legs blown off doesn't have to 'deal with it'. They have to live with the way they are, faced with the knowledge that their life has changed and will never be the same again. The shock stays with me, the pain, accompanied with this growing awareness of depression. A therapist would deduce that this is part of the process of grief, the gate before us that some pass through and go forward. I don't know. This is how it is for me. I'm not following any known path, just my heart.

The searing sense of loss goes deeper than I can express. It has never left me. It distinguishes me in a way I can't explain. This season of grief has become the defining experience of my life.

CHAPTER 12

# Birthday Surprise

*2013...*

On Jessica's 28th birthday, in February 2013, I finally found courage to go through all the materials about her that I had stored in the IKEA cabinets near my desk. I couldn't face this before because it meant accepting what had happened.

There were cards and letters, drawings, books, some just scribbles on scraps of paper, other more formal documents. I saw the card that she had given me for Father's Day in 2006. The jolt of the discovery shook me. Jessica wrote:

> 'Dad – you are my hero and my inspiration. I just hope you knew.'

In my youth, I had many dreams and ambitions. In Jubilee Campaign, I came on my mission, my calling. But after reading her words, it became evident that it would be my family and friends who would remember me. I reflected on my mother; such a significant influence on me. Her greatest accomplishment was her life.

And it became clear what my legacy would be.

Joan had given me the privilege of signing Jessica's birth certificate in 1985. The official document had a box to tick: 'Qualification?' I wrote 'Father.' That meant everything to me. It confirmed my identity and pointed to my legacy: a proud father to three amazing children, and now grandfather to three – so far – grandchildren.

At 21 years old, Jessica affirmed this when she placed that card in my hand. That was my accomplishment.

When I think of Jessica and see her photograph or unexpectedly find something that belongs to her, I get that special feeling inside, that movement in my heart. It takes me a few seconds to steady myself. It was just that way, when I opened an unmarked envelope and discovered a lock of her hair. It was like touching her. It was treasure in my hand. The shock caused me to cry out.

Over a thousand and eight hundred days had passed but I was still in a state of shock. I couldn't accept her loss. I couldn't find that entry (or exit) point that said: acceptance. This was to be a never-ending journey. But the instant those words appeared, I questioned if writing that sentence had been a kind of acceptance, or a starting point of that acceptance.

\* \* \*

My friend Roley's husband Michael Horowitz was a former state prosecutor in Israel and had served during the trial of Ivan Demjanjuk (featured in Netflix's documentary series *The Devil Next Door*). Michael's mother, Marion Bienes, was a Holocaust survivor of Westerbork and Bergen-Belsen concentration camps.

She recorded her experiences in *Why the Horses? An Autobiography of Marion Bienes.*[1]

Her book title evoked the moment when the parting of the Red Sea saved the children of Israel, but she posed this question: the Pharaoh's avenging soldiers were drowned. But why did their horses perish? Why were the animals punished? She wrote

> And no assistance whatsoever could be expected from outside, not even professionals like for instance psychiatrists. Having had no previous experience in treating concentration camp survivors they were at a loss what to do or say for many years to come; and complicating the matter was the fact that all of us, who survived one or more concentration camps, buried our memories, experiences and feelings as deeply as possible – not only because we tried to forget, no everybody around us also wanted to forget. By-and-by of course we realised that forgetting was impossible – learning to live with it was the principle thing to do. And that could take years, often a lifetime.

Of course, it's impossible to make comparisons with Mrs Bienes's experience. But her stark frankness after such a calamity spoke to me. At the time, I wasn't in a place to think that anything could help or that I would ever heal.

---

1. Marion Bienes, *Why the Horses? An autobiography of Marion Bienes* (The Netherlands: Horowitz, 2012), 117

I liked the King James translation of Ecclesiastes 3:11: 'He has made everything beautiful in its time. He has put eternity into man's heart yet so he cannot find out what God has done from the beginning to the end.' The New English Translation gives this alternative: 'God has made everything fit beautifully in its appropriate time.'

This Scripture explained that God has hidden things, everlasting things, that we can't understand about the past or the future. But at some point, we'll know, and when we do, the design will be unveiled; within that, the beauty will be ours to affirm and to claim, as our heritage.

The Scripture didn't make me feel any better, but it was something I came to believe. Yet, the question that couldn't be extinguished was simply: why has this happened?

Joan's prophetic word about Gideon came to me. Gideon was forthright in his challenge: if the Lord is with us, why have all these bad things happened to us . . . ? God did not offer Gideon explanations or promises or even comfort. Just this: 'Go in the strength you have . . . am I not sending you?'

I liked the way Rick Warren, the pastor of the Saddleback Church in California, expressed it: 'We don't need an explanation. We need the presence of God.'

\* \* \*

As I was nearing the end of this book, I embarked on a personal audit: what place had I reached on my journey? Had anything changed?

There were things that helped. Some like driftwood came to my side and gently nudged me, held me afloat.

When I lay crushed by the earthquake that had come on me, there were flashes from the rescue mission, like torch lights amidst the dust and ashes, hands lifting bricks and mortar and rubble off me. But the weight was too great, the pain too intense. I couldn't move. I don't know when that lifted. But something in the atmosphere changed. That's when the torch shone brighter through the fuzzy smoky haze.

I recognized the movement and mercy of God that reached out to me, arranged situations and people and moments and cards and music and dreams and messages and books and the touch of a child's hand . . .

I started this book to try to find some explanation or comfort or closure (a word I dislike) or framework to understand what had happened. But as I excavated the anatomy of this experience, I wondered if that was possible. In factual, objective terms, the absence of life is when life leaves the body. But how to solve this mystery? How can I understand or explain this event that is inexplicable?

George Verwer's words resonated when we talked. He didn't tell me everything would be OK. That I had to trust and have faith. This was someone who opened his heart and acknowledged that there were things he didn't understand. He led me to explore the 'mystery of spirituality' in a way that I could make it my own. I guess for me, that will have to do. That's as much light as I have at this junction of the journey.

\* \* \*

When we were first married, I discovered that Joan had a vivid imagination that exploded in her dreams.

Over morning coffee, Joan would tell me of her nightly exploits. She was a fantasy figure, flying through the air. She was a conqueror, sword in hand, vanquishing foes. Once she was Sean Connery. Or was it Sean Connery's father? After we'd laughed about her escapades, she'd turn to me. But my dreams were forgotten by morning. I had almost nothing to contribute. And that's how it had been since childhood.

Sometime after 2007, that changed. This time, the dreams stayed with me. The dreams were of Jessica.

When I was dreaming, I knew I was enveloped in a dream. In the dreams, I told myself to memorize what Jessica looked like: the length of her hair, the clothes she was wearing. She appeared both young and old. She was dancing, swaying. In another one, she had short hair. In one dream, I saw her in profile as she passed me. She wore a dark maroon long-sleeved shirt, loose, flowing; it was tucked into greyish, dark-coloured trousers, also loose and flowing. She seemed to be floating. She looked elegant and stylish, as she always did. Her hair was long, streaming, past her shoulders, down her back, pinned at the sides. But when she was dancing and pulling faces, she was wearing different clothes, something beige and flecked, layered, like the dress I recall when she was young, with a white silky long-sleeved blouse.

One time, her hair was long, rolling everywhere. She looked beautiful. I knew it was a dream. I knew that she had passed from the world I lived in. And so did she. We were together in the dream. We both understood what had happened. And something passed between us. I don't know what it was. Something secret, something mysterious, that only she and I shared. A private joke, as we often had, in the living world.

I was determined to remember this dream. And as I was moving from dream to consciousness, I spoke the details to my waking mind.

In one dream, she told people where she was about me, that I looked after her. Then she embraced me. That dream had such power and vibrancy that I thought it had really happened.

In many of the dreams, I was desperately sad, weeping, as were many of the people who appeared in them. It was evident to every character in the dream that our sadness was caused by her loss. The sadness became a regular feature in these nocturnal encounters.

On 20 March 2011, I knew I was in a dream with Jessica. She appeared to be luminous and floating. There was something radiant and sparkling about her and where she was. She looked dazzlingly beautiful. Her eyes were playful, she was laughing and dancing with that special chuckle. We were near an exquisite palace. She was in a group but left them and came to me. For a few moments, we were the only two people outside the palace. She was excited and spoke in a voice I recognized, 'Dad, I've got something for you.' Somehow, I was moving away from her. It wasn't difficult or painful, just something we both realized would happen. She would be inside; I would be outside. Then she told me, 'I'm going to watch you from the window at the top. I'll hold it out for you. You'll know it when you see it. I'll wave from the window, so you'll know it's me.'

On Sunday 2 August (2015), Joan and I were awake but drowsy. She marshalled resolve and went downstairs to feed Indy and get our early morning drinks. I offered no resistance. The clock on her bedside table read: 6:55am. She returned at 7:15am with two steaming hot mugs of green tea. In the 20 minutes she was out of the room, I had fallen into a deep sleep, and awoken only when I heard her in the room. I was emerging from an intense dream.

I was in an ancient building in a room with wood-panelled walls like those in Parliament. Someone spoke of Jessica and I felt tears in my eyes. I became aware of someone in the room and saw him in profile. I asked a question, and he answered me. He touched my arm, 'I know how you feel.' His voice was soothing, and I had the feeling that he truly understood everything about me, my anguish. He was gentle, with a kind face, and his presence calmed me. I asked who he was and reached for my notebook to write down his name. He replied, 'You know who I am.' Sorrow had covered me like a cape, but after he spoke, my heart was comforted. In my dream, it was a significant moment.

I kept notes of the dreams. I'd awaken and scribble key words onto the nearest magazine or paper. Later in the day, I recorded the dreams with as much detail as I could remember. I locked this away in the secret tower of my memory.

\* \* \*

In January 2014, I returned to India with Joan. We arrived on a midnight flight from London Heathrow. Devaraj, his wife, Lathija, with their daughters, Dawn and Deborah, were waiting for us at Mumbai's international airport as we stepped into the hot steamy Indian night. Standing alongside them were Asha, her husband and son. Devaraj had become one of my closest friends. In 1996, I'd started out thinking that I was helping with this work to rescue children from Mumbai's red-light district. But my life was enriched beyond measure, both by Devaraj, and the close relationship that had developed with some of the Jubilee children.

It was an emotional reunion because it connected me with people who were important to me and a mission that had become the driving force in my life. Devaraj always referred to 'our children'. Over the past years, he'd arranged for the children to phone and Skype me. Now they were grown, and appeared as confident, beautiful young women.

Some girls had made friends with Rachel during the week she'd spent at the Jubilee Homes as a teenager, while others told me that they remembered Jessica. One girl said, 'I want you to stand with me as a father when I get married. You must be there.' She didn't have a wedding date or a husband in mind; when she noticed my hesitation, she insisted. 'Promise me!' (Three years later, it was a joy to share the honour with Devaraj as together we walked her down the aisle.) Later, I saw Prem, the young boy that Jessica had taken to her heart at the shelter, who'd been near death. If ever there was a 'miracle boy', Prem was the one.

It was Joan's first visit to India. The affection of everyone we met, and the intoxicating charm of the country won her over. 'I love India!' she told anyone who would listen. The only place she struggled was in crossing the street, with traffic hurtling forward in every direction.

We'd gone to India for the opening of BTC's Academy, a school for 'our children'. Devaraj had dreamt of such a resource for years. 'I want our children to have the best education possible. We must create an environment where they can excel.'

The Academy was a large, impressive building near the new Jubilee Home, about two hours outside Mumbai. We'd established the first Jubilee Home in 1996 in the countryside amidst lush green rolling hills. When first built, both homes (known as Jubilee One and Two), stood tall as the only high-rise buildings on the horizon. Twenty years later, property tycoons had erected tower blocks almost everywhere, some within a few feet of our homes. With reduced privacy and increased concern for the children's safety, there was only one option: move. The new Jubilee Home was a large purpose-built construction on three floors.

The girls had moved in December 2013, but there was to be a formal opening of the new home on the same day as the inauguration of the Academy. The Academy had only recently been completed so everything looked clean and fresh. 'Your dream came true,' I said to Devaraj, and gave him a hug.

Over one hundred children crammed into the Academy's main hall and their excitement spread to the many guests and local politicians who applauded their musical performances and amusing dramas. Sir Ewan Harper of the Laing Trust, generous benefactors, concluded the proceedings. With the formalities over, about thirty of the dignitaries, church leaders and senior staff were directed outside. I'd assumed we were heading to the new Jubilee Home, but instead we were guided along the side of the Academy towards the main entrance of the property.

We walked beside an elevated level where shrubs, plants, seedlings and ferns had been planted in neat rows in the freshly worked earth. It looked impressive, but I was concerned that we were bound for an unknown destination in the crisp afternoon sun. I followed the group until Devaraj stopped at one corner near the main gate. He asked Joan and me to step forward.

I noticed a wooden sign covered by a cloth. He pulled the fabric back. The words 'Jessica's Garden' had been crafted into a stylish wooden sign nestled amidst a range of freshly planted bougainvillea plants. Jessica's Garden ran to about sixty foot by forty foot, and covered the entire front and one side of the Academy.

'Jessica's Garden is the first thing people will see when they arrive,' Devaraj told us. 'Jessica will always be remembered here.'

The surprise of this evocative and poignant gift ripped through me. Joan was equally stunned. I struggled to find words. The only expression I could offer was a monsoon of tears. The pent-up intensity of the past few years, coupled with our visit to such special friends, erupted with explosive emotion. Devaraj and a few of the church leaders prayed for us, and there were hugs and tears from many.

The Jubilee Homes and the shelter in Mumbai had always been one of my favourite places in the world. Now they would become one of the most unforgettable.

Devaraj and his family opened their hearts to us, and I would never forget them.

\* \* \*

Four months later, Ben Beecroft asked me to give St Paul's an update about Jubilee Campaign. I prepared a Power Point presentation about India and included a photograph of Jessica at the shelter crouched over Prem. I knew this would increase the pressure on me when I spoke.

It was a warm sunny Sunday in May. Joan took Seth to the creche so that Rachel and Matt could attend the service together. They sat in the third row with Eden, a toddler, on her mother's lap.

The worship music finished, and then it was my turn. I spoke about the rescued children and Jessica's experience caring for Prem. The image of Jessica with Prem appeared on the overhead screen. At that moment, I caught some movement near me.

Eden had climbed down from Rachel's lap and walked down the left aisle. Then, she appeared at the front row. She looked cheekily at me, her eyes twinkling. It must have taken courage to leave the security of her parents, in an unfamiliar location, and to step up to the front of the church. But she'd seen me and decided to come to me. Eden disregarded what else was happening around her. Her grandad was at the front. She decided to reach out to him, to tell him something, to show him something: Grandad. Look. I can walk. I did it all by myself.

At a time when I was struggling with memories from the past and how to live with them, my granddaughter was saying to me – let's make new memories in the future.

For Eden, it was a moment of character and courage. For me, it was to become an enduring memory of the start of a reconciliation with the past. And there were new memories to be made with Seth, and Lily.

Seth gave me a small red bus and we played with it. His invented game made no sense, and had zero chance of securing investment on *Dragon's Den*. But it caused Seth great hilarity.

One afternoon when Luke and Lily visited us, she gathered daisies from the garden and brought them to me. Her heartfelt gesture moved me.

It was true. Through such encounters, new memories were being formed. And the memories were good. I yearned for more of them.

Seven years had passed since the tumultuous and traumatic event of 27 December 2007. Seven years seemed to me a significant passage of time. I expected something to happen, a turning point when things shifted. But it came to nothing. And as the last days of December drew near, I acknowledged that there wasn't going to be an ah-ha moment. Still, something felt different. Perhaps the trip to India, the encounter with Eden at church, amongst others, had contributed.

\* \* \*

When driving in Addlestone, I took longer complicated routes to avoid passing Green Lane Cemetery because I could never drive past the gates without going in. But on Saturday, 27 December 2014, that was my destination. I parked near the chapel at the entrance and took the first pathway towards the far end of the cemetery.

My heart felt heavy. I hated this place. I hated that I had to walk this path. At that moment, I recognized that my footsteps were taking me to the exclusive location on this earth that had become the resting place, a kind of home, to the physical body of my beloved daughter. And in that second, the hate that I felt turned to a strange form of love, as if a new paradigm was unfolding.

I walked forward carrying the sadness attached to this place but equally the love that had caused me to make this journey.

As I approached Area 25, I noticed that people had placed trinkets, traditional Christmas ornaments and other seasonal ornaments on tombs. One grave had an Emirates Stadium banner with football memorabilia. The items seemed out of place. Who will see this? What was the point? The response again was immediate. These decorations were visual demonstrations that loved ones weren't forgotten. Each one lived on in the memory of others. The departed shared a part of their life in the living world.

When I reached Jessica, it seemed as if time took on new meaning. It didn't matter if I stayed with her for a few minutes or an hour. Normal rules didn't apply. Natural time was replaced by a moment of perception that did not belong in any other category of life. So, time holds no place in this patch of earth. She remained here. That was my total knowledge. There was nowhere else I would rather be. There was nothing that meant anything to me. What could there be? All that people like me – those who proudly bear the badge of mourners – had in this world was in this place. And in places like this. The memory of our loved ones burned like a flame for those whom we honour with our presence.

And so it was for me, Green Lane Cemetery on Addlestone Moor would always be remembered as a field of memories.

\* \* \*

Two months later, on 27 February 2015, I was preparing to return to Green Lane Cemetery to mark Jessica's thirtieth birthday.

I assembled everything the night before: a crimson coloured scented candle, two bouquets of blue lilies, and a silver gas-filled balloon with sky-blue text that declared 'Happy Birthday' to the world.

Luke had moved into a flat in Byfleet, about three miles away, and dropped in after leaving Lily at nursery. He had developed a passion for coffee. He had freshly roasted coffee beans from South America and other exotic locations delivered directly to his door. He'd brought along a few pods for us and it wasn't long before the intoxicating aroma of coffee filled the house. He chided me for reaching for the jar of instant.

We sat at the dining-table by the patio doors. His coffee tasted good, but I particularly savoured being with my son. There wasn't anything particular to discuss, but rather the casual enjoyment of shared affection.

Luke picked out a melody on the guitar. He was self-taught but had a good command of the instrument. Joan and I loved to hear him play as the acoustics carried the rhythms and sounds of his music through the house.

After about an hour together, I said goodbye to Luke and Joan and headed to Green Lane. The car park was empty. I was pleased to be the only visitor.

I carried everything to The Place. I tied the silver birthday balloon to a post that served as a holder for a tea-light candle. Next, I set the crimson candle in the centre of the heart-shaped black marble memorial. There was a particularly strong breeze and it took some persuasion for the flame to catch. We had two vases, so I filled both with water, then did my best to arrange the flowers. The blue lilies made a terrific contrast to the yellow roses that I'd taken two weeks earlier on Valentine's Day. The red roses that Joan had brought the day before were fresh, and the splash of colourful flowers contrasted well with the black stone.

I noticed that the lilies were dipping into the path of the candle, so I crouched down and rearranged the stems of the blue flowers. It didn't quite work and took a few attempts to get them looking right – and safe from the flame of the candle.

Suddenly I felt a physical tap on my back.

I was stunned. I spun round. No one.

The Happy Birthday helium balloon had wound tightly around the post as it swayed furiously in the breeze. It brushed against me and bumped forcefully into me again and again. It was as though someone was holding the balloon and repeatedly bouncing it into me.

It took a few seconds to realize the breeze had caused the balloon to crash into my back while I was leaning over to attend to the flowers. Before I could move, I started to laugh. It was just the kind of cheeky thing

I could expect. It didn't lift the sadness, but I found myself smiling through the tears.

It was just the balloon. It was just the breeze. But for a few minutes it shook me.

* * *

That dark December day in 2007 was a memory that didn't fade. I remembered every moment in forensic detail.

That night, I had been restless and couldn't sleep. None of us could. It was 4:30am when George Verwer came to my mind. Joan was curled up under the blankets. I moved quietly to the table near our bed. The glare from the computer's monitor was the only light in the corner of our bedroom. My fingers moved across the keyboard. I tried to frame words into the saddest email I would ever write to him.

My beloved daughter Jessica . . .

George awoke early that morning in his home, 60 miles away, in Kent. He read Scripture for a while, then checked his emails. He wrote: 'There were about 50-some new ones . . . I saw your name & felt that must be the first I open. I have no words . . . I would phone you right now but it's very early . . .'

His second email expressed sympathy but really there were no words to say.

George prayed for thousands of people around the world and used photographs as a reminder. He had more than 150 photo albums stacked neatly on bookshelves in his home office. A day or so after he received my message, he noticed that one of his photo albums had become wedged behind a cabinet. He thought it unusual and couldn't recall how it had been separated from the others. He stretched out to extract it but as he retrieved the album, it fell on the floor. It flipped open on a page with a photograph of Jessica. George took it to Drena, his wife, and said, 'Look, that's Jessica.'

I told the story of George's photo album in my eulogy at Jessica's memorial service in January 2008. I aimed this at people who were struggling, not those who were strong. To those who felt far from home, in a place they shouldn't be; who got stuck somewhere, couldn't get out, couldn't get away; who had been knocked down, maybe got knocked out; bruised, battered by life, damaged, wounded, shot down; hurt, badly hurt, hurt beyond repair . . . who had almost given up, when faith and hope seemed out of reach like a rider far in the distance but our voice too feeble.

When I first heard the story of the photo album, I took it as something mysterious and unfathomable. But later, a new meaning came to me.

Jessica had faith and was baptized by choice. She talked with me of her spiritual journey over lunch at the Harvester in Ottershaw in 2005. But her struggles with mental health issues in the last short period of her life left her troubled and distressed. Yet, she reached out even during this period of her internal turmoil. She and Rachel attended church together in the last few months of 2007. During our last extended time together (on Christmas Day) Jessica asked if we had *The Message Bible*. We didn't. She told me we should get one, she wanted to use it.

I was heartened by the incident of George's album. It was a truth that became alive in our heart. The photo album was lost, somewhere it shouldn't be. George found it and took the album to its rightful place, alongside the other albums. I thought this was a way of us knowing that the Lord had taken Jessica home. It was a precious gift to our family. A glimmer amidst the darkness of winter.

\* \* \*

Rachel took Seth and Eden to St Paul's and she signed up for the Alpha course. Alpha had started in 1977 at an evangelical Anglican church in London but by 2015, over 27 million people worldwide from many denominations had completed the ten-week programme. Taking Alpha crystallized Rachel's thinking; it drew her to a personal faith, and she was baptized at St Paul's in July 2015.

During an Alpha away day, Rachel felt a calling on her life. Beyond the important role within her family, she felt urged to play a part in Jubilee Campaign.

Rachel donated by standing order every month to Jubilee Campaign. She started the practice of giving in childhood; I still have the envelope she'd handed me, when she was about ten, with a 20p coin saved from her pocket money. As a teenager, she spent a week at the Jubilee Homes in India and became a pen-pal with one of the girls; at 17, she completed a sponsored sky-dive to raise funds for an Aids Orphans Home that we'd hoped to start. Her sky-dive was phenomenally successful and raised over £300,000. The money came from our supporters, matched funding from the Laing Trust, and a similar amount pledged by Jubilee Campaign USA. The money enabled Devaraj to buy land, and build, furnish and pay three years' operating costs for the new home: Jubilee 4.

All this had happened while teenage Rachel struggled with chronic fatigue syndrome (ME), an illness she battled for three years. Despite this, she completed her National Vocational Qualification in Childcare from Brooklands College. Her courageous spirit triumphed and eventually she overcame the serious illness and took up work at the Sure Start Centre in Weybridge.

Rachel had this quality of grace that made people want to do things for her. But it would be wrong to mistake kindness for weakness. She combined steely determination with clear thinking; an ability to focus on priorities. It was these characteristics that enabled her to accomplish so much. Equally, she wasn't afraid to change her mind and say, 'Actually . . .'

I knew she had a burning heart of compassion. But I questioned if office life would hold her interest. With Seth at school, and Eden attending a local nursery, Rachel had two free mornings a week. She'd completed work experience at the school where Seth started; the head teacher recognized her gifting and offered her an immediate job. Matt acknowledged Rachel's greatest desire was to establish a family home with children of her own. He encouraged her to pursue her dream, without pressuring her to return to work. I knew that extra finances would come in handy so was surprised but delighted when she turned them down and chose to volunteer with us. Matt was already a volunteer – updating our outdated systems and providing technical support when we needed it.

Rachel and Matt were a perfect match. Their locked hearts spoke to a love that ran deep. The closer Joan and I got to Matt, the more we admired him. There was a strength to his character and an excellence to the decisions he made. He guarded Rachel and Seth and Eden to ensure no harm came to them. There wasn't anything he wouldn't do for them. When, we were together, it seemed like he'd always been part of our family.

* * *

We gave Rachel an overview of Jubilee Campaign's current activities. She quizzed us on Jessie's House in Zimbabwe.

Bill Hampson's charity, the Epiphany Trust, employed a young Zimbabwean, Eddie Mubengo, and suggested that our organizations partner together and set up a day-care centre using Eddie's network in his home village of Muzondo. The project started with 70 orphaned and vulnerable children, many from child-headed households. Bill wanted to lift us and called it Jessie's House.

'Why haven't you told supporters about it?' Rachel asked.

'We don't have good images,' was my feeble reply.

She immediately started problem-solving. She identified a photographer, commissioned his assignment, and organized his trip to Zimbabwe. It was a tour-de-force performance and demonstrated her skills and resourcefulness. Rachel's choice of photographer couldn't have been better. Soren was the son of Janet and Craig Rickards. He lived in France and worked as an extreme-sports photographer capturing daring stunts around the world. Soren had that casual style and gentleness that won friends easily.

A few months later, we waved him goodbye at Heathrow Airport, bound for Harare via Paris and Dubai.

In Zimbabwe, Soren and Eddie Mubengo's brother hired a 4x4 Toyota, and headed out to Jessie's House in Muzondo, a remote village too small to feature on any map and hours from the nearest highway. We'd paid for a bore hole that delivered clean water to the village for the first time – the biggest event in their history. About three thousand within a four-mile radius benefitted from the well, and people came out of their homes to thank Soren.

One day while travelling on the highway they stopped to give a lift to a woman. She'd been walking for hours with an empty container to draw clean water for her family.

The incident on the highway reminded me of something Jessica told me after returning from Zimbabwe. They'd been driving in the interior and picked up someone desperately ill from the roadside. I remember her saying, 'I don't think he survived. I don't even know if he was alive while he was in the car with us.'

The details are hazy. But the passion in Jessica's voice stayed with me. I recognised the same intensity when she spoke of wanting to work at the Jubilee Homes in India, and of visiting Fr Shay in the Philippines.

When Seth and Eden started school, Rachel formalized her role with Jubilee Campaign. She quickly grasped how the organization functioned; her natural leadership ability and strong communication skills confirmed we'd made the right decision. And she was bursting with ideas.

Her first suggestion was to develop an educational programme that used phonics as a way of teaching English to vulnerable children in rural communities who felt they were left behind, with little hope of lifting themselves out of poverty. It has terrific potential and there was genuine interest from potential users.

I look forward to the hour when Rachel appears. I hadn't imagined that I would be handed this privilege of time together as father-and-daughter.

Rachel's gift has been to make me feel uplifted after spending time with her.

* * *

Rachel was teaching Seth and Eden to pray and told me that three-year-old Eden's first prayer was for me: that my hat wouldn't fly off. I needed her prayers. It had caused great hilarity when they heard I'd slipped on the ice causing my hat to blow away.

Eden spent Tuesday afternoon with me while Rachel took Seth for swimming lessons. In July 2015, Eden and I were on the sofa watching an episode of *Peppa Pig*. She saw an image of Jessica on a shelf above the television and asked who it was. I told her, 'It's your aunty Jessica.' 'Oh,' she said, and she repeated her name: 'Aunty Jessica.' I told Eden that she was named after Jessica. She spoke the name aloud, 'Jessica,' in her tender baby voice.

Later that afternoon, Eden returned for a second unexpected visit. She saw my photograph of Jessica in her scarlet red prom dress, and asked, 'Is that me?'

I told Rachel about the incident. She texted me that evening:

> Oh wow! We talk a lot about Aunty Jessica and look at photos of her. The one in her red dress is on our dining room window, perhaps she recognized it from there? I always want them to know about Jess and we talk about her most days. Yeah, I have ever since Seth was little. I always want them to know her. I just say things about when mummy, Uncle Luke and Aunty Jessica were kids and stories from when we were younger etc so they are used to me talking about her normally. But Seth knows that she died. I just say it's very sad and we all miss her. Seth often says he will meet Aunty Jessica in heaven!
>
> I just make sure she's used to hearing Jess's name when I talk about the family.
>
> Of course, it's painful but better than her not to know about Jess.

Someone had written to me after December 2007: 'The pain helps us to recall the love.' I never fully grasped the significance of that sentence but understood it when I read Rachel's message. Her words resonated. It reminded me of something I think I'd heard somewhere: Learning to live amongst the living is part of the journey of healing.

Seth and Lily and now Eden were gifts from God. Their arrival in our lives carried their legacy, because as children and grandchildren, they would bring healing to our family – and to me.

# Conclusion

Some light fires to the past desperately trying to forget, others light candles desperately trying to remember.

I started writing this without knowing if I could complete it or if it would be shared with anyone else beyond our family and friends who walked with us in the days after 27 December 2007. I wanted to preserve the memory of Jessica, but at times, even the mention of her name made me pause to catch my breath, and occasionally gave me a sensation of vertigo. But I remained in pursuit because I wanted to celebrate her life and not be choked by the pain of her loss.

I thought of it as a way of saying 'Goodbye Jessica'. But even those two words are painful to write.

I always hated saying goodbye to Jessica. When she packed her little red Rover Mini for the long drive to university in Manchester, I stood on the pavement and watched her car till it reached the end of the road, turned left onto Queen Mary's Drive, heading for the M25 motorway. I waited until she was out of sight. I then waited for the text that would follow, hours later: 'I'm here. Love you Dad. Jx.' She knew I wanted to hear she was safe.

But I took the journey into the past, stumbled across incidents that were hidden, almost forgotten. Things that once had made things special and given meaning to my life.

Early on it became clear that this wasn't going to be a guidebook or a triumph of the spirit reflection, or an uplifting inspirational testimony because I thought it could encourage others who had been felled by such great hurt, or bring comfort – dare I say hope – to those who mourned, by understanding their heartache. Therapists and counsellors help many. I held no such aspirations. Every wound is different. But our wounds shape our lives. Until you are damaged, it's hard to understand. My wound was too personal, too painful, too deep, for me to consider anything else beyond my sorrow.

One afternoon in 2017 as spring turned to summer, friends were visiting when Luke dropped in with Lily. At some point, I heard her say, 'I really miss Aunty Jessica.'

There was a melancholic spontaneity about how she expressed herself. Janet Rickards was the first to respond, 'We all miss her, Lily.'

When I started writing, I didn't know how long it would take or where it would take me. But after hearing my granddaughter, I was determined to push through and reach a conclusion, whatever that was to be.

I understood that Lily and Seth and Eden had listened to stories about their Aunty Jessica from her brother and sister. Still, I wanted them to hear another voice: a father remembering his daughter. I had so much to tell them, yet I wondered if there would ever be a perfect day or the right time for all that I yearned to say. So, my prayer is that one day, through the pages of this book, they will know something of her footprint on this earth. And be inspired.

But I wrote it also for myself.

I wrote it to return to that moment of her birth, those hours when my heart was bursting to tell people of her arrival. That I had become a father, that the world was new, and I was being remade, reborn. Now, I wanted to tell people of her adventures and achievements, her struggles, and her pain – her life.

And I wanted all who pass this way to know just what an amazing person she was, how I loved her, and how I miss her.

I walk on and find things to do with a renewed significance of time:

> To be with Joan, my best friend. I never want to be far from her and today we are closer than we have ever been. Her sacrifice and devotion to our family humbles me.

> To watch Rachel fulfil the role she was born to play as a mother and homemaker with her strong yet sweet husband Matt; Matt, a tower by her side, a strength and comfort by ours. Rachel and I have evolved a new relationship working side by side on Jubilee Campaign. I feel like it's a prize I've won. I'm energized by her dynamic character and inventiveness. It sharpens ideas and stretches her imagination to find new ways to strengthen our mission to help Children at Risk.

> To drive to Walton with Luke to catch a late-night movie or stay with him awhile, drinking coffee, listening to his guitar. My heart swells with admiration and respect: he faced his challenges and

overcame them, to emerge with quiet humility as a man of depth and character, and a devoted father. We stand together as father and son. That means everything to me.

To relish time with our grandchildren: captured by the bounding exuberance of Lily; engrossed by Seth who speaks with the wisdom of the ages; and with Eden, who welcomes me as her friend and speaks this way to me – a true joy at this point of my life.

Meeting family and friends recalls times past with hopes high of things to come.

And these moments build new memories within.

I had kept everything that belonged to Jessica, her room unchanged. I guarded that space, holding on to the way things used to be. But it couldn't remain that way. Joan and I knew that we had to deal with her worldly possessions, and our own. Better us, than Rachel and Luke being left to deal with stuff, when we're no longer on this earth.

It's said that the journey of a thousand miles begins with the first step. In January 2018, we took that first step.

We started with a box of toys and souvenirs from Jessica's childhood, tucked away in the depth of the loft. A selected few were placed in a memory box. Others could be let go. Before that, I took each item, and held it in my hand, recalling the times it had been in play when she was young. Then I set it down. I learned this from *döstädning* (in Swedish) or death cleansing, a system of shedding unnecessary things. Death cleansing gave me a structure to grasp what was required of us.

I never thought I could let go of Jessica's belongings. But when that moment came, I found courage to embrace it. There were tears, of course. But there was also a release. The moment of saying goodbye to Jessica's things held some particular power of mystery. Now, having made a start, we go forward.

I listened to the messages of sages and of Scripture. Things I've known before, I come to understand, as if for the first time. Perhaps, the time was right for me to hear them now, in this season. Previously, the soundless noise of sorrow blocked everything else out.

I wanted to lay down the past.

But the past rises up and appears like a castle under siege with arrows of memories suspended in space, ready to fall at any time and pierce this wounded heart. I can never get over the past or escape or evade the shadow that falls. Still, I am finding strength day by day, to walk through the past with the help of God our Father, my Father. The unfailing love of God reaches out to me. While faith starts to glow again in my heart.

I no longer fear the past and have made my peace with all that happened.

I am ready for the future.

I am seeking the presence of God rather than an explanation of the tragedy that overshadows my life.

I am making new memories to give the past meaning.

I am learning that grief is the price we pay for love.

I have accepted that the mystery of spirituality influences the way ahead.

I am exploring what it means to be living with mystery.

The discovery I have made is that her memory doesn't fade. In a way I can't explain, she is always there, her presence abides with me still. I hold this sense of her voice and her spirit in my heart. The longing and aching of past times haven't diminished but the memories have become lighter to carry.

That day, 27 December 2007, defines me. It changed me, as did her birth, twenty-two year earlier.

These words of valediction, from a father to his beloved daughter, has affirmed to me that my journey is destined never to reach that station when I can speak these words:

Goodbye Jessica . . .

# Epitaph

Jessica considered everything of mine as hers. Things would disappear: a particular pen or a hand-made paper notebook. At times, it was maddening. I'd spend ages searching for the object. At some point in the hunt, I'd walk into her room, and find it there. If I questioned her, she'd give me that look. A raised eyebrow. A glint in her eye. A glance that sliced the air between us. That special signal shared between father and daughter. I knew. And she knew.

Jessica created a folder on my computer. She used it for various things including her CV; she'd message me or call and ask me to add something.

The folder was titled: Jess.

Sometime after 2007, I saw the folder. Still, it took me a long time to open it. When I summoned up the courage, I found two documents I had never seen before. One was titled 'God', the other 'But As For Me'.

## *God*

Psalm 9:1-10 (NIV 1984)

I will praise you, O LORD, with all my heart;
I will tell of all your wonders.
I will be glad and rejoice in you;
I will sing praise to your name, O Most High.

My enemies turn back;
they stumble and perish before you.

For you have upheld my right and my cause;
you have sat on your throne, judging righteously.

You have rebuked the nations and destroyed the wicked;
you have blotted out their name for ever and ever.

Endless ruin has overtaken the enemy,
you have uprooted their cities;
even the memory of them has perished.

The LORD reigns forever;
he has established his throne for judgment.

He will judge the world in righteousness;
he will govern the peoples with justice.

The LORD is a refuge for the oppressed,
a stronghold in times of trouble.

Those who know your name will trust in you,
for you, LORD, have never forsaken those who seek you.

## *But As For Me*

Job 19:25–27 (NLT)

But as for me, I know that my redeemer lives, and He will stand upon the earth at last. And after my body has decayed, yet in my body I will see God! I will see Him with my own eyes. I am overwhelmed at the thought.

We set up charitable tributes in Jessica's memory to complete her unfulfilled desire to help vulnerable children, and the profits from this book will be dedicated to these projects.

Jessie's House in Zimbabwe has grown in influence and effectiveness. It is transforming lives in this remote village. The day care centre developed into an infant school, while Jessie's House Farm with its innovative solar drip irrigation system feeds 160 children every day, and the surplus of food is given to the elderly and disabled in the village. In the Philippines, Fr Shay Cullen took The Jessica Smith Scholarship Fund to great success: over 200 Filipino students completed their higher education; there are now several teachers, caregivers, office employees in various jobs as a result. Later, The Jessica Smith Training Centre was established. In India, Jessica's Garden blossomed. The remarkable partnership with Reverend Devaraj has seen many children rescued, and lives changed, and our relationships deepened with many children from the Jubilee Homes and the shelter in Mumbai.

All donations to Jubilee Campaign.

Contact danny@jubileecampaign.co.uk

Danny Smith
Jubilee Campaign
PO Box 700
Addlestone
Surrey KT15 9BW
United Kingdom

www.jubileecampaign.co.uk
and  www.goodbyejessica.com